PLANT FAMILIES
How To Know Them

Illustrated keys for determining the families of nearly all of the members of the entire Plant Kingdom.

by

H. E. JAQUES
Professor of Biology
Iowa Wesleyan College

Published by the Author
Mt. Pleasant, Iowa

The Pictured-Key Nature Series

"How to Know the Insects," Jaques, 1941
"Living Things—How to Know Them," Jaques, 1940
"How to Know the Trees," Jaques, 1941
"Plant Families—How to Know Them," Jaques, 1941
"How to Know the Spring Flowers"
(To be published in 1942)
Other Subjects in Preparation

In Both Spiral and Cloth Binding

Send all orders to

H. E. JAQUES
709 N. Main
Mt. Pleasant, Iowa

PLANOGRAPHED BY
JOHN S. SWIFT CO., INC.
ST LOUIS-CHICAGO-NEW YORK-CINCINNATI
PRINTED IN ST LOUIS, MISSOURI, U S A.

INTRODUCTION

WHEN life and living things are considered, nothing else is so basic as the plants. All other life is directly or indirectly dependent upon the green plants for sustenance. An intimate knowledge of plants is necessary for many vocational fields. Culture demands some knowledge of plants. Everyone may find interest and relaxation in studying or associating with them.

The total number of plants known to science is so great that a lifetime would scarcely suffice for one to learn to recognize all of them. The family, which is an aggregation of similar plants, makes a unit highly important for study. The number of families in the plant kingdom is sufficiently small that with a reasonable amount of study one can place most of the plants he sees anywhere in their proper relationship and understand them much better. In our judgment, no other division offers as good possibilities for a broad general understanding of plants and animals as the family group. It is for this reason that this book has been written.

The Pictured-Key Nature Books are not based on new research. The effort instead has been to take the important facts of plants and animals and to make them more understandable for the beginner and all students who appreciate clarity. In "Plant Families" all groups of plants have been considered and one or more plants used as examples of each family. Species of plants commonly seen have been chosen wherever possible for these examples. Some families of small consequence have been purposely omitted in the interests of making the keys easier to handle. With such a large field to cover, space has not permitted much to be said about any one plant. When the student finds himself especially interested in some particular group of plants, he will need to refer to one of the many excellent books on the group of his choice.

Many good friends have helped us. Professor Henry S. Conard of Grinnell College, whose studies of Mosses are well known, has written the keys for the entire division Bryophyta. Arlene Knies, Mabel Jaques Cuthbert, Francesca Jaques and our good neighbor, Betty Laird Swafford have made most of the drawings. It's grand to have faithful friends; we want to thank them all.

Mt. Pleasant, Iowa,
November 15, 1941.

THE FAMILY PICNIC

CONTENTS

SOME PLANT FACTS

was in his counting house, counting out his money." Kings have not always given their first attention to the welfare of their subjects.

Man is "king" of all the animals. He writes the books and says so. But there are no plants which publish claims to authority, so it may be a question just which one heads up the Plant Kingdom.

That doesn't matter anyway for his subjects really count for more than a king. In this case there are 250,000 different kinds of subjects, but no one has ever tried to even guess how many individuals.

We took a census once of just the trees growing in Mt. Pleasant,--an unusually nice little town. They added up 15,998 individual trees. We would have been crazy, of course, to have attempted to count the dandelions or the grass plants, or the bacteria. A project like that might help solve the unemployment problem of the post war period.

So much for random thoughts. Since there are some important things that should be said about plants, we'll get on to a few of them.

PLANT REQUIREMENTS

Moisture, an acceptable temperature, and for most plants, soil and sunlight are necessary for their growth. Where all of these conditions prevail in highly satisfactory degrees, plants are most abundant and at their best. In moist tropical areas plants if left to themselves grow into the nearly impenetrable jungle. Once the jungle growth is removed and such an area set with useful plants, the yield may be prodigious.

Temperate regions for part of the year are too cold or may have such limited rainfall as to support only a fair plant coverage. Deserts have everything else, yet grow but little for want of moisture. The seas have the moisture and usually the food materials and sufficient warmth. In their upper strata the water courses often produce a prolific plant growth but fail at greater depths through being unable to meet the light requirement. As the poles are approached, temperature becomes the limiting factor and plant life while present, is greatly reduced in size and in numbers of species and of individuals.

SOME EARLY PLANTS

Plants are age-old. Even at the dawn of the Cambrian period-- some would say nearly a billion years ago--many of the simpler plants had made a good start. Ferns have been on the way perhaps half a billion years while flowering plants have likely been beautifying the world with their blossoms and fragrance for more than fifty million years. Plant styles have undergone many changes through these long ages and numerous species have flourished for a time and then become extinct. Abundant fossil remains reveal vegetation growths that in some ways greatly out-stripped the best we know today.

PLANT FREEDOM

The green plants live an independent life. With the sunlight for a motive force, they combine the carbon dioxide of the air with water to form much of their tissues. With a few more elements taken from the soil, they are self sufficient.

Other great groups of plants have been "on relief" so long as to lose their chance of independence. Now with their chlorophyll gone, they must live as parasites or saprophytes and like all the animals are directly or indirectly dependent upon the green plants for food. The green plants then become king of all living things.

LARGE AND SMALL PLANTS

Plants on the whole display a wide range of sizes. Some bacteria are so small that more than six thousand billion would be required to fill a cubic inch of space. At the other extreme, vines occasionally exceed a length of one thousand feet. Now and then a tree may be over 300 feet high with a trunk more than 30 feet in diameter. One tiny bacterium would have about the same size ratio to the big tree as a well fed house-mouse would have to the entire earth and all that is in it.

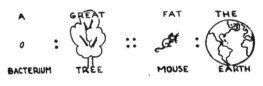

PLANT PROJECTS

The best way to know and understand plants is to live with them. For the student, some collecting or research project if thoughtfully pursued is sure to pay well in pleasure and knowledge. "How to Know the Trees" suggests 25 tree study projects (p. 13) while in "Living Things—How to Know Them" a chapter is entitled "More than 100 Suggestions for Nature Study Projects" (p. 7). These offer many good suggestions to which the ingenious teacher or student can readily add other good ones.

COMMON VS. SCIENTIFIC NAMES

Plants that have common everyday uses or relationships are known by "common names". In fact, many of them have several common names and that is how the trouble begins. For instance, Abutilon theophrasti, a widely distributed and all too abundant Asiatic weed, is referred to by the following, Velvet leaf, Indian Mallow, Butter-print, Button-weed, Pie-print, Mormon-weed, Cotton-weed, Indian Hemp, Sheep-weed, American jute, Pie marker,

6

etc. If a plant is cosmopolitan each language may also have one or more names for it.

To make the confusion still worse the same name is frequently applied to several different plants, leaving the hearer in doubt as to which one is meant.

To ease this difficulty, Linnaeus, a Swedish naturalist around 1760, devised a system of scientific names which would be world wide in their application. He did such a good job that his scheme is still in use, and while it is not perfect the plan of having one universal scientific name for each plant has many advantages over common names.

Some violets are yellow, some purple, some white; some are large, others are small; the leaves are sometimes deeply cut and some are not cut at all. There are so many differences among the

THE VIOLET FAMILY

violets that many kinds ("Species" is a better word) are recognized. All of these are enough alike in some essential characters that they are unmistakably related. Each one shows its relationship to its group. Such an aggregation is known as a genus and is given in this case the name <u>Viola</u> which is the Latin word for violet. Just as the Smiths have their John, William and Mary, so there are <u>Viola</u> odorata, <u>Viola</u> pubescens, <u>Viola</u> pedata, <u>Viola</u> tricolor, and many others. These scientific names are made up of a Latin noun the genus. It is always capitalized. The word following is the species and is a Latin adjective modifying the generic noun or a noun in apposition with it. The species name often reveals some important character of the plant. Thus the four violets named above are respectively, very fragrant, have hairy stems, have leaves resembling a bird's foot, or are variously colored (pansy). The word or abbreviation following the species is the "authority" or "author" and tells what scientist proposed this scientific name. Zoologists have ruled that all species names begin with a small letter; some botanists prefer to follow that same plan. Scientific names are underscored or printed in italic type.

A few basic plant facts have been quickly mentioned. There is much to be known about plants and many excellent books to tell it. The reader whether a beginner or one who has long loved plants is wished a continuing of happy experiences with these, our faithful friends.

SOME HELPFUL BOOKS

A small book like Plant Families, at best, can present only a general view of the entire plant kingdom. If one becomes especially interested in any particular group of plants he will need to refer to books that specialize in his chosen field. Some highly useful ones are suggested below, but this list must not be thought of as being at all complete. The attempt has been only to include manuals useful in identifying plants.

ALGAE

"The Fresh-water Algae of the United States", G. M. Smith
"The Green Algae of North America", F. S. Collins
"Cryptogamic Botany", Vol. 1 Algae and Fungi, Smith

"Algae, the Grass of Many Waters", Tiffany
"The Algae and their Life Relations", Tilden

FUNGI

"Bacteriology", Tanner
"The Fungi Which Cause Plant Disease", Stevens
"Agaricaceae of Michigan", Kauffman
"Mushrooms, Edible, Poisonous, etc.", Atkinson
"Manual of the Rusts in the United States and Canada", Arthur
"The Biology of Bacteria", Henrici
"The Lichen Flora of the United States", Fink
"The Myxomycetes", Macbride & Martin

"Manual of Vegetable Garden Diseases", Chupp
"Elements of Plant Pathology", Melhus & Kent
"Introduction to Plant Pathology", Heald
"Principles of Plant Pathology", Owens
"Filterable Viruses", Rivers
"One Thousand American Fungi", Chas. McIlvaine
"Mushrooms and Toadstools", Gussow & Odell
"The Mushroom Book", N. L. Marshall

MOSSES AND LIVERWORTS

"Mosses with a Hand-lens", A. J. Grout
"Mosses with Hand-lens and Microscope", A. J. Grout

"Hepaticae of North America", Frye & Clark

FERNS

"Ferns of North Carolina", Blomquist
"Ferns of the Northwest", Frye

"Ferns of Tropical Florida", Small
"Guide to Eastern Ferns", Wherry

FLOWERING PLANTS

"The World of Plant Life", Hylander
"Wild Flowers", House
"Hortus", Bailey
"Flora of the Prairie and Plains of Central North America", Rydberg
"Wild Flowers Worth Knowing", Blanchan
"Manual of the Grasses of the United States", Hitchcock
"Illustrated Flora of the Northern United States and Canada", Britton & Brown
"How to Know the Trees", H. E. Jaques
"Illustrated Flora of the Pacific States", Abrams
"Manual of Botany", 7th Edition, Asa Gray
"Field Book of American Wild Flowers", Mathew F. Schuyler

"Manual of Cultivated Plants", L. H. Bailey
"Flora of the Southeastern United States", Small
"Flora of the Rocky Mountains", P. A. Rydberg
"Field Book of Western Wild Flowers", Armstrong
"Wild Flowers of California", M. E. Parsons
"Plants of Iowa", H. S. Conard
"Manual of Weeds", Ada Georgia
"Key to Some Common Weeds", Paul B. Mann
"Field Book of American Trees and Shrubs", M. F. Schuyler
"Handbook of the Trees of the Eastern United States", R. B. Hough
"Trees and Shrubs of the Rocky Mountains", Burton O. Longyear
"Field Manual of Trees", John H. Schaffner

HOW TO USE THE KEYS

The use of keys for identifying plants and animals dates back many years. The addition of pictures to supplement the keys is more recent and makes their meaning clearer. The use of keys is much like traveling a strange region where the road intersections are well marked. If the traveller reads the signs intelligently and follows their instructions, he should have no trouble. A little understanding of terms and the use of care in selecting the right direction each time should find the correct family to which the plant belongs.

It will be noted that the key statements are set in opposing pairs which are numbered alike but lettered differently. We find a toadstool in our front yard and wish to know to what family it belongs. With specimen at hand we start at page 10 and compare la with lb. Noting that our specimen has no flowers, true roots, or leaves, we try "Division Thallophyta, p. 10".

This time we find three statements to be compared (1a, 1b, and 1c); 1b fitting the case shows us our specimen belongs to the Fungi on page 47 and we compare 1a and 1b to select 1b and go as directed to number 2 where 2b is seen to be right and we then consider 21 to se-lect 21b and then 22b, 60b, 64b, 65b, 67b successively. Finally 69b reveals that our specimen belongs to the "Family Agaricaceae". Now if we will go back through the keys noting the facts that lead us to our decision, we will have a good technical description of the Agaric mushrooms.

Near our toadstool may grow a dandelion and we wonder about its family. Beginning again at page 10, 1b, 2b, and 3b send us to the seed bearing plants, page 89, where it is found to be an Angiosperm (1b) and a Dicotyledon (4b). On page 100 we select 1b then go in turn to 25b, 105b, and 106a to learn that the pesky dandelion is associated with the asters, daisies, and sunflowers in the great family Compositae.

In the back of the book we find that a list of the families of plants arranged according to their relationship begins at page 151. If each plant studied is checked in this list and its relatives noted, the student will get a better concept of the plant kingdom, as well as having a graphic record of his progress.

PICTURED-KEYS FOR IDENTIFYING THE FAMILIES
OF THE ENTIRE PLANT KINGDOM

There are more than 250,000 known species of plants. A life time of specialization would be needed to know most of them intimately. But these many species fall into a few hundred families.

An earnest student or careful observer can acquaint himself with so many of these families that he will recognize the relationships of the majority of the plants he sees, no matter how widely he travels. The family makes the best unit for a thorough general knowledge of plants or animals.

To secure a clear picture of the plant kingdom it is necessary to begin with the larger groups. The reader will now gather up his equipment of keen eyes, alert mind, and good perseverance and he is ready to start on a most fascinating journey through the Kingdom of Plants. 'R you ready? Let's go!

KEY TO THE PRINCIPAL GROUPS OF PLANTS

The plants are usually divided into four great groups. It is commonly recognized that some of these groups are "artificial". The Thallophyta in particular includes many plants which are somewhat alike in their simplicity but which are evidently widely disrelated.

1a Plants without distinction of root, stem and leaf; without flowers, both aquatic and terrestrial; algae; fungi, and lichens. "HAVE NO ARCHEGONIA". Figs. 1 to 200.
Division THALLOPHYTA p. 10

1b Plants with distinct leaves; with or without roots or flowers. 2

2a Small plants (to 4 or 5 inches tall) with green or gray-green leaves, or tiny leaf-like forms on damp earth or floating on water. No true roots or flowers. (Some small oval green discs floating on quiet water with roots suspended beneath are flowering plants and do not belong here.) "HAVE ARCHEGONIA BUT NO VASCULAR BUNDLES". (Mosses and Liverworts.) Figs. 201 to 253.
Phylum BRYOPHYTA p. 70

2b Plants with true roots and vascular bundles; mostly with veiny leaves 3

3a Plants without flowers or seeds, herbs (not woody), propagated by spores. Figs. 254 to 265.   "HAVE VASCULAR BUNDLES BUT NO SEEDS". (The Ferns, etc.)
Phylum PTERIDOPHYTA p. 86

10

3b   Plants with flowers (sometimes very simple; one tiny stamen or one pistil may constitute a flower) and seeds. "HAVE SEEDS". Figs. 266 to 472. (The seed-bearing plants.)
Phylum SPERMATOPHYTA p. 89

THE THALLOPHYTA

1a   Plants green, with chlorophyll, thus organizing their own food by photosynthesis. Figs. 1 to 116.
Sub-division PHYCOPHYTA, The Algae . . 2

1b   Plants without chlorophyll (not green). Living parasitically on living plants or animals or as saprophytes on dead, organic matter. Figs.127 to 200. Sub-division MYCOPHYTA, The Fungi p.47

1c   Dual organisms in which a green plant species (alga) is held in parasitic embrace by a species of fungus. Usually gray-green or yellow-green but sometimes displaying bright colors. Common on tree trunks, rocks and often growing directly on the ground. Figs. 117 to 126.
The Lichens p. 44

⇥ KEYS TO THE FAMILIES OF THE ALGAE ⇤

2a   Plant cells without recognizable nucleus or plastids. Coloring matter (usually blue-green) diffused throughout the cell. Figs. 1 to 9. (The Blue-Green Algae) 3

2b   Not as in 2a. Plant cells with distinct plastids and of various colors and shapes 10

⇥ THE BLUE-GREEN ALGAE (MYXOPHYCEAE) ⇤

3a   Unicellular or colonial in habit; never forming filaments. Reproduction vegetative only. Figs. 1 and 2. 4

3b   Cells forming definite filaments, but no endospores. Figs. 5 to 9. 6

3c   Cells usually growing on other plants; solitary, colonial or forming small filaments. Forms endospores. Figs. 3 and 4 . 5

ORDER CHROOCOCCALES

4a   Cells always in colonies which grow prostrate upon rocks or other bodies and which have erect column like outgrowths. Largely marine.
Family ENTOPHYSALIDACEAE

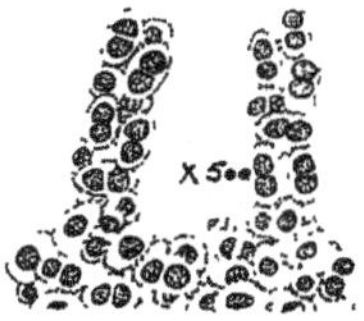

X 5••

Figure 1

Fig. 1. Entophysalis magnoliae Farl.
    The family is largely marine though some species grow in fresh water. Rocks between the tide lines form the favorite marine habitat.

4b   Cells solitary or in colonies but never with column like outgrowths.
Family CHROOCOCCACEAE

11

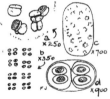

Figure 2

Fig. 2. a, <u>Chroococcus</u> <u>turgidus</u> Nag.;
b, <u>Merismopedia</u> <u>punctata</u> Mey.; c, <u>Syne-chococcus</u> <u>aeruginosus</u> Nag.; d, <u>Gleocapsa</u>
sp.

Many known species of diverse form make this a large family. The numerous tiny free floating species make an important group in water contamination.

ORDER CHAMAESIPHONALES

5a   Thallus multicellular as a result of cell division. In spore formation an entire cell is completely divided into endospores.   Family PLEUROCAPSACEAE

Figure 3

Fig. 3. <u>Hyella</u> <u>fontana</u> H.& J. a, vegetative thallus; b, cells forming endospores.

There are a few fresh water forms but most of them are marine. For the most part they grow attached to other plants.

**5b   Cells solitary although often many growing close together. Spores cut off at end of cell one at a time.
                                   Family CHAMAESIPHONACEAE**

Figure 4

Fig. 4. <u>Chamaesiphon</u> <u>incrustans</u> Grun.

Rather common as an epiphyte on larger freshwater algae. Most of the family are marine species.

ORDER HORMOGONALES

6a   Thallus a filament of uniform diameter except possibly the terminal cells may be smaller. There are no heterocysts (empty cells). Several filaments often bound together with a sheath.   Family OSCILLATORIACEAE

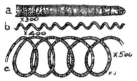

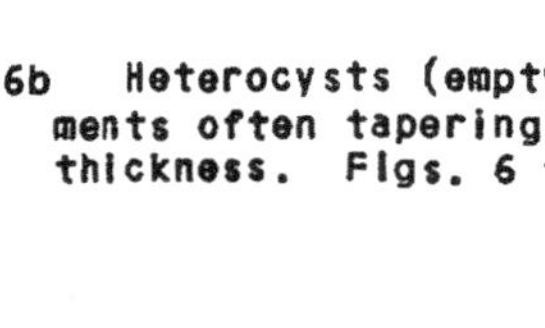

Figure 5

Fig. 5. a, <u>Oscillatoria</u> sp; b, <u>Spirulina</u> <u>major</u> Kutz.; c, <u>Lyngbya</u> <u>contorta</u> Lemm.

This plant is a classic among the "blue-greens". Its "oscillations" consist of moving the tip of its filament in a circle. Many folks do but little better.

6b   Heterocysts (empty cells) present in the thallus. Filaments often tapering whip like though sometimes of uniform thickness. Figs. 6 to 9. 7

12

7a Filaments branched. Figs. 8 and 9 9

7b Filaments unbranched. Figs. 6 and 7 8

8a Filaments nearly the same diameter throughout; covered
  with a gelatinous sheath.   Family NOSTOCACEAE

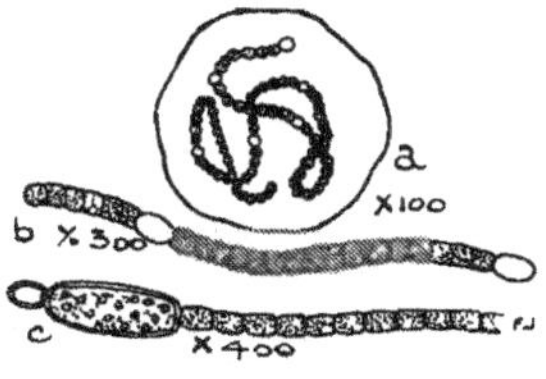

Figure 6

Fig. 6. a, Nostoc sp.; b, Anabaena sp.;
  c, Cylindrospermum sp.

The pale blue-green gelatinous bean-
sized colonies of Nostoc are sometimes
found in great abundance in clear
spring-fed lakes. If they could be kept
permanently they would rival pearls for·
beauty.

8b Filaments gradually tapering to one or both ends.
                    Family RIVULARIACEAE

Figure 7

Fig. 7. a, Sacconema rupestre Borzi.;
  b, Rivularia sp.

Colonies of Rivularia are often arranged with the basal ends of the filaments standing at the center of a
sphere and the whiplike ends radiating
to the circumference. Such balls are
frequently 2 or 3 mm. in diameter.

9a Filaments with false branches; enclosed in a sheath.
                    Family SCYTONEMATACEAE

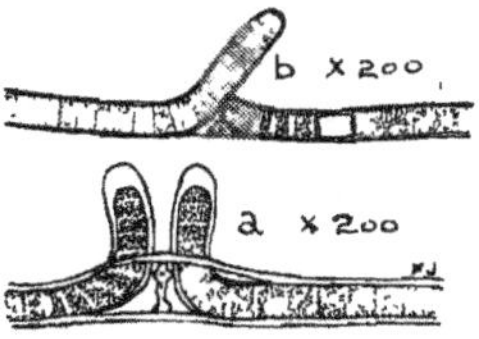

Figure 8

Fig. 8. a, Scytonema sp.; b, Tolypatrix
  sp.

False branching is characteristic of
several groups of algae. It's something
like propaganda or stealing 2nd base;-
you must look close to see exactly what
goes on.

9b Filaments with true branches; sheathed; often more than one
  cell in diameter.   Family STIGONEMATACEAE

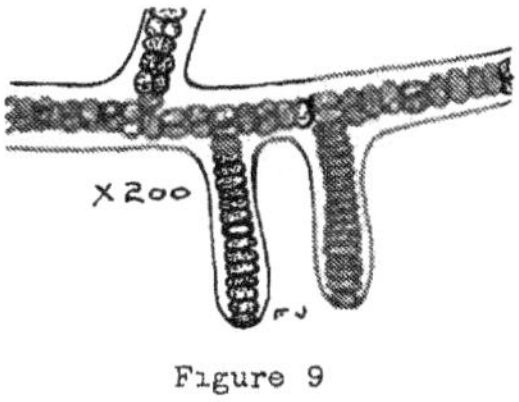

Figure 9

Fig. 9. Stigonema turfaceum Cooke.

The members of this genus grow in damp
soil or in fresh water and are fairly
common.

10a Algae that are bright "grass-green" in color. Figs. 10
  to 52 11

13

10b Algae with red, brown or yellow pigments more or less mask-
ing the green chlorophyll. Figs. 53 to 116 48

11a Plant fine; relatively small. Figs. 11 to 52. 12

11b Plant coarse, at least a few inches long, branched, with
nodes from which arise whorls of cylindrical leaves which in
turn bear leaflets; sometimes encrusted with lime.

Order CHARALES
Family CHARACEAE

Figure 10

Fig.10. *Chara fragalis* Derv. a, branch
of plant; b, reproductive organs.

This is the only family of its order
and class and has comparatively few
species though they are fairly common
and widely distributed. These plants
are so different from all other green
algae that they have been given a phylum
of their own. These plants attain a
height of several inches and are quite
complex in their structure. Reproduction is always sexual. *Nitella* is another common genus.

12a Naked free-swimming cells with one, two or rarely more whiplike flagella at the anterior end. Some species are colonial.
(Some have a non-motile encysted stage.) Sexual reproduction
unknown. Figs. 11 to 14. 13

12b Microscopic single celled plants to large thallus-like
plants with cellulose walls. The flagella of motile forms
usually number 2 or 4, and are equal in length. Most species of
the phylum have sexual reproduction. Figs. 15 to 52. 16

ORDER EUGLENALES

13a Cells non-motile and living attached to crustaceans and
rotifers in indefinite masses or branching colonies.

Family COLACIACEAE

Figure 11

Fig.11. *Colacium calvum* Stein. a, colony;
b, rather rare temporary motile stage.

This family is sometimes assigned to a
separate order. And some college students
think they invented hitch-hiking. Even very
simple plants like these have been at it for
millions of years.

13b Vegetative cells unattached and swimming by means of one or
more flagella. Figs. 12 to 14. 14

14a Cells usually with green chloroplasts; if colorless an eyespot is always present, the same as in the colored species.
Sexual reproduction is unknown.   Family EUGLENACEAE

14

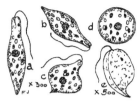

Figure 12

Fig.12. a, b, c, _Euglena viridis_,-changing forms of active cell; d, encysted cell which will live through drought or low temperatures; e, Phacus acuminatus Stokes.

These highly interesting forms often become exceedingly abundant. They may be suspected by the very bright shade of green covering the pool of water.

14b. Cells colorless and having no eyespot. Figs. 13 and 14. .15

15a Cell with a pharyngeal rod (elongated structure near base of flagellum). Family PERANEMACEAE

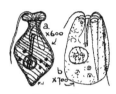

Figure 13

Fig.13. a, _Urceolus cyclostomus_ Mer.; b, _Entosiphon sulcatum_ Stein.

Some species of the family have but one flagellum; others have two in which case one extends ahead and the other trails.

15b Cells without a pharyngeal rod. Family ASTASIACEAE

Figure 14

Fig.14. a, _Astasia dangeardii_ Lemm.; b, _Menoidium incurvum_ Kleb.

Flagellated animals of this type usually pull themselves through the water instead of carrying the flagellum behind as might be suspected.

⇥ THE GREEN ALGAE (CHLOROPHYCEAE) ⇤

ORDER SIPHONALES

18a Tubular free-living algae, somewhat branched. Sexual reproduction by non-motile eggs which are retained after fertilization within the oogonium. Both aquatic and terrestrial species. Family VAUCHERIACEAE

15

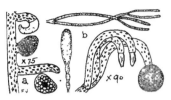

Figure 15

Fig.15. a, Vaucheria sessilis
D.C. with reproductive organs;
b, Dichotomosiphon tuberosum
Ernst.

The first species is often to be
found thickly covering flowerpots,
greenhouse beds or smooth damp
ground in garden or field. It has
been termed "green-felt".

18b A branching tubular thallus, parasitic within the leaves of plants of the family Araceae or the tissues of some mollusks.
Family PHYLLOSIPHONACEAE

Figure 16

Fig.16. Phyllosiphon arisari Kuhn. a, filament; b, leaflet of Jack-in-the-pulpit
with diseased spot.

19a Thallus without septa, the erect pinnately branched part at-tached by a prostrate rhizome. Gametes for reproduction are produced in the pinnate branches. Along both our Atlantic and Pacific coasts.
Family BRYOPSIDACEAE

Figure 17

Fig.17. Bryopsis corticulans Setc.

Reproduction seems to be much more active in the
spring.

19b Much-branched tubular thallus with gametes born in special-ized organs.
Family CODIACEAE

Figure 18

Fig.18. Codium fragil Hariot. a, portion of
plant; b, two gametangia.

All species are marine and many are limited to
the warmer seas.

20a Vegetative cells motile by means of flagella (some have non-motile resting periods). Figs. 19 to 24. 21

20b Vegetative cells not self-moving. Reproductive cells often motile. Figs. 25 to 52 25

ORDER VOLVOCALES

21a Motile cells always solitary. Figs. 19 to 22. 22

21b Motile cells in colonies. Figs. 23 and 24 24

21c Motile cells in one genus solitary and in the other colonial but distinguished from 21a and 21b by having many contractile vacuoles near the surface and processes of protoplasm extending to the wall.   Family SPHAERELLACEAE

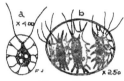

Figure 19

Fig.19. a, Sphaerella lacustris Wittr.

Common in stone or earthenware cavities periodically filled with rain water.

b, Stephanosphaera pluvialis Cohn.

Ornamental urns in cemeteries are recommended as a likely place to look for Sphaerella. If that seems gloomy try a park; its the urn rather than the cemetery that counts.

22a Motile cells with no enclosing wall. With 2-4 or rarely 8 flagella and one eyespot.   Family POLYBLEPHARIDACEAE

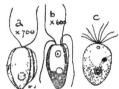

Figure 20

Fig.20. a, Stephanoptera gracilis Smith; b, Pyramimonas tetrarhynchus Schm.; c, Polyblepharides fragariiformis Hazen.

An eyespot is always present in active individuals.

22b Motile cells with an enclosing wall. Figs. 21 and 22. . .23

23a Wall consisting of two overlapping halves which push apart in reproduction.   Family PHACOTACEAE

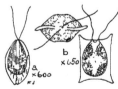

Figure 21

Fig.21. a, Phacotus lenticularis Stein; b, Pteromonas aculeata Lemm.

These plants are surrounded by overlapping cells, somewhat similar to the diatoms.

23b Wall continuous and not divided. With two or four flagella but never more.   Family CHLAMYDOMONADACEAE

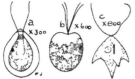

Figure 22

Fig.22. a, <u>Chlamydomonas gloeocystiformis</u> Dill.; b, <u>Platymonas elliptica</u> Smith; c, <u>Brachiomonas submarina</u> Bohlin.

A large family with several common species.

24a Colonies forming either a hollow sphere or a flattened plate. The individual cells and usually the colony embedded in gelatin. Family VOLVOCACEAE

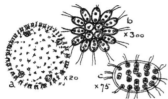

Figure 23

Fig.23. a, <u>Volvox aureus</u> Ehr.; b, <u>Gonium pectorale</u> Muell. c, <u>Pleodorina illinoiensis</u> Kof.

<u>Volvox</u> is well-known in theory as it is often described in books on biology. It is sometimes very abundant in permanent bodies of quiet water.

24b Colonies solid, made up of layers of four cells each. No gelatinous covering. Family SPONDYLOMORACEAE

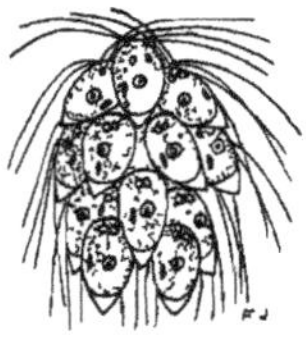

Figure 24

Fig.24. <u>Spondylomorum</u> sp.

Such minute algae as we are now considering may appear in great abundance and shortly seem to be wholly gone only to reappear when conditions are again favorable.

25a Usually spherical or ovoid cells held together in colonies by a gelatinous secretion in which the cells are embedded. These gelatinous colonies take various shapes and sizes. Figs. 25 to 28. 26

25b Plants not forming gelatinous colonies. (A few members of the Chlorococcales are an exception). Figs. 29 to 52. 29

ORDER TETRASPORALES

26a Cells attached by a stem which may be slender or broad and short. Solitary or in dendroid colonies. Family CHLORANGIACEAE

18

Figure 25

Fig.25. a, <u>Stylosphaeridium stipitatum</u> G.& G.; b, <u>Malleochloris sessilis</u> Pash.; c, <u>Prasinochladus lubricus</u> Kuck.

The last species mentioned is marine.

26b Cells not attached as in 26a. Figs. 26 to 28. 27

27a Vegetative cells with two or more long pseudocilia at their anterior end. Usually in microscopic or larger colonies.
                                        Family TETRASPORACEAE

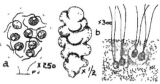

Figure 26

Fig.26. a, colony of <u>Apiocystis brauniana</u> Nag.; b, colony and small part of <u>Tetraspora</u> sp.

These are found in quiet waters. Some are ephiphytic.

27b Without pseudocilila. Figs. 27 and 28 28

28a Gelatinous sheath surrounding colony the same throughout; cells usually elongate.   Family PALMELLACEAE

Figure 27

Fig.27. a, <u>Palmella miniata</u> Lieb.; b, <u>Palmodictyon viride</u> Kutz.; c, <u>Gleocystis gigas</u> Lag.

A few members of this family grow out of water but most of them are aquatic.

28b Gelatinous sheath of each cell usually distinct; cells mostly spherical.   Family COCCOMYXACEAE

Figure 28

Fig.28. a, <u>Coccomyxa dispar</u> Schm.; b, <u>Elkatothrix</u> spp.

Found in abundance among the floating vegetation in lakes, etc.

29a Single celled plants or multicellular colonies, but never forming filaments. (The water net [Fig. 35] is not a true filament). The cells take many unusual shapes. (A few colonies are embedded in a gelatinous mass; and another few expanding into a thallus). Figs. 30 to 37 31

29b Plants highly multicellular, leaf-like or developing into hollow tubes or solid cylinders. Figs. 29, 38 and 39. . . . 30

29c Not as in 29a or 29b but developing into a branched or un-branched filament. Figs. 40 to 52 38

30a Chloroplasts star-shaped; reproduction only by non-motile asexual spores.

Order SCHIZOGONIALES
Family SCHIZOGONIACEAE

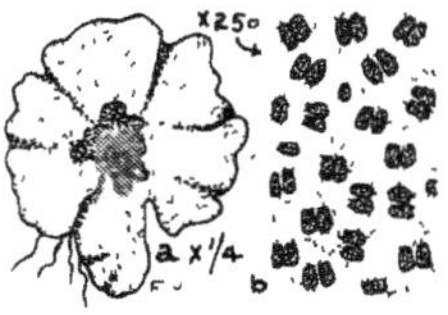

Fig.29. Prasiola mexicana Ag. a, thallus; b, magnified surface view.

Some marine species belong here but the majority are inland forms.

Figure 29

30b Chloroplasts not star-shaped; reproduction by zoospores and by motile isogametes. Figs. 38 and 39 37

ORDER CHLOROCOCCALES

31a Cells solitary. Figs. 30 to 33 32

31b Colonies of a definite number of coenobic cells. Figs. 34 to 37 35

32a Elongated cells attached by a short stalk. Essentially sol-itary, though many plants often grow crowded together in a ra-diating cluster. Usually multinucleate. Reproduce by zoo-spores and by gametes, both biciliated.   Family CHARACIACEAE

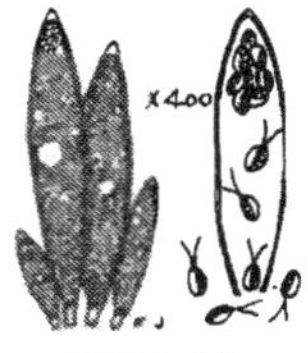

Fig.30. Characium angustatum Br.

Grows attached to other algae, or upon stones or submerged wood.

Figure 30

32b Not attached as in 32a. Figs. 31 to 33 33

33a Cells multinucleate, spherical to elongate, often bearing an elongated root-like process. Reproduction by biciliated zoospores or gametes.   Family PROTOSIPHONACEAE

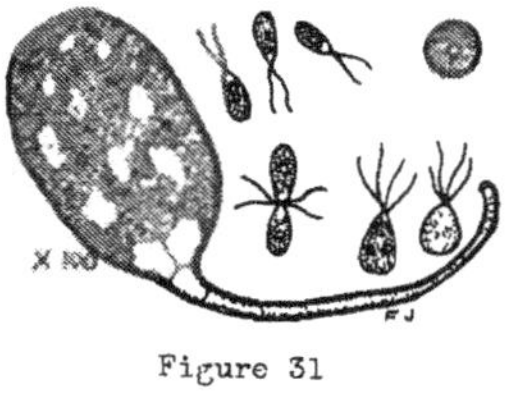

Fig.31. Protosiphon botryoides Klebs.

Common on moist soil; often mixed with Botrydium with which it may be easily confused. Protosiphon contains starch; Botrydium never does; a starch test will settle any uncertainty.

Figure 31

20

33b Cells with but one nucleus. Figs. 32 -and 33. 34

34a Cells small, usually somewhat spherical, often variously
   ornamented but always rather symmetrical in shape. Aerial or
   aquatic, nucleus haploid.   Family CHLOROCOCCACEAE

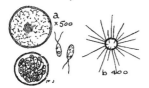

Fig.32. a, Chlorococcum humicola Rab.;
   b, Golenkinia radiata Chod.

Often very abundant on damp soil and
brickwork and in soil. A few species are
aquatic.

Figure 32

34b Cells larger and unsymmetrical in shape. Usually found on
   or within other algae. Some species parasitic. Nucleus
   diploid.   Family ENDOSPHAERACEAE

Fig.33. Kentrosphaera bristolae Smith.
   This is a soil-living species.

Figure 33

35a Solitary or colonial; when colonial, irregular with no fixed
   number of cells. Reproduction only by autospores (formation
   within the parent cell of several walled spores having the
   shape of the parent cell and which on release grow to its
   size). (A large family including many species of widely diver-
   sified shapes.)   Family OOCYSTACEAE

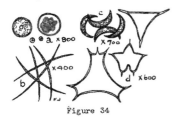

Fig.34. a, Chlorella variegatus Bey.;
   b, Ankistrodesmus falcatus Ral.;
   c, Selanastrum sp.; d, Tetraedron
   spp.

Chlorella is interesting in that it
frequently inhabits the tissues of
animals in a cooperative way or as a
·parasite. The family is a very large
one.

Figure 34

35b Colonies of definite arrangement. Figs. 35 to 37 36

36a Colony with an unchanging number of cells throughout its
   life; formed by the swarming of zoospores within the mother
   cell or other vesicle.   Family HYDRODICTYACEAE

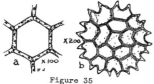

Fig.35. a, Hydrodictyon reticulatum
   Lag. Water net; b, Pediastrum
   boryanum Men.

The net of Hydrodictyon takes an
elongated sack-form, sometimes reaching a length of a foot or more.

Figure 35

21

36b Unit, a colony formed by the union of autospores after their
liberation. Number of cells from 4 to 128.

Family COELASTRACEAE

Figure 36

Fig.36. Coelastrum microporum Nag.

It is an inhabitant of fresh-water lakes.

36c 2-4 or 8-cells (occasionally more) each with single nucleus
arranged parallel, radially or in other definite form.

Family SCENEDESMACEAE

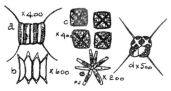

Figure 37

Fig.37. a, Scenedesmus quadricauada
Breb.; b, Scenedesmus obliquus
Kutz.; c, Crucigenia quadrata
Mor.; d, Tetrastrum elegans Pla.;
e, Actingstrum hantzschii Lag.

This rather large family takes
many forms. The algae scoured from
the walls of fish bowls often belong here.

ORDER ULVALES

37a Mature thallus a solid cylinder several cells thick.

Family SCHIZOMERIDACEAE

Figure 38

Fig.38. Schizomeris leibleinii Kutz.; a, cross
section; b, longitudinal view of part of
thallus.

Usually in clear water; not abundant but widely distributed.

37b Thallus a hollow tube, or ribbon-like, or flattened leaf
like. In each case the wall only one or two cells thick.

Family ULVACEAE

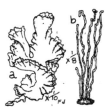

Figure 39

Fig.39. a, Ulva lactuca L. Sea Lettuce;
b, Enteromorpha intestinalis Grev.

Sea lettuce attains a height of nearly a
foot. Its vivid brilliant green makes a
sharp and pleasing contrast to the brown and
red algae with which it grows.

38a Zoospores and male reproductive cells with a ring of many
flagella at apical end. With apical caps indicating where cell
division has occurred. Filaments simple or branched.

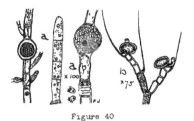

Figure 40

Order OEDOGONIALES
Family OEDOGONIACEAE

Fig.40. a, Oedogonium spp.;
b, Bulbochaete mirabilis Wit.

These are naturally attached
plants though broken parts or even
large masses are found freely
floating. A basal cell develops a
holdfast for attachment.

38b Zoospores with two or four flagella. Filament simple or
branched (only a singular spherical cell or irregular colony of
such cells in Protococcus). Figs. 41 to 49. 39

38c No zoospores. No flagellated reproductive spores. Reproduction by a zygospore formed by the union of two non-motile
cells. Filament always unbranched. Figs. 50 to 52. 46

39a Cells with but one nucleus and one chloroplast. Figs.
41 to 47 40

39b Cells with more than one nucleus and with several discoid
chloroplasts. Figs. 48 and 49 45

ORDER ULOTRICHALES

40a Cells solitary, in irregular groups or in plate-like
colonies. Figs. 44 and 45 43

40b Cells in colonies of branched filaments. Figs. 46 to
49 44

40c Cells in colonies of unbranched filaments. Figs. 41 to
43 41

41a Filament wall composed of a series of overlapping H-shaped
pieces. Chloroplast lobed but often indefinite as to shape.
Family MICROSPORACEAE

Figure 41

Fig.41. Microspora willeana Wittr.;
a, filament; b, zoospore and
H-pieces; c, aplanospore being
released from filament.

These plants are at their best
in the spring where they are common
in small quiet waters.

41b Without H-pieces in wall of filament. Figs. 42 and 43. . 42

**42a Each cell of filament enclosed in its own cellulose wall
making the filament wall appear stratified.**
                          Family CYLINDROCAPSACEAE

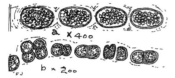

Figure 42

Fig.42. Cylindrocapsa geminella
 Wolle.; a, young filament;
 b, older filament.

Try pools and ditches in late
spring if you wish to find it.

**42b Filament wall not stratified, the single chloroplast plate-
like and lying near the cell wall.   Family ULOTRICACEAE**

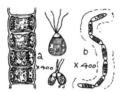

Figure 43

Fig.43. a, Ulothrix zonata Kutz.; b, Geminella spiralis Smith.

These plants are normally attached and may
be very abundant in slow-running water.

**43a Cells solitary or sometimes in irregular masses of 2 to 50
cells. No zoospores or gametes known.   Family PROTOCOCCACEAE**

Figure 44

Fig.44. Protococcus viridis Ag.

Very common on tree trunks, etc.
This and a few other species are distributed world-wide.

**43b Part or all of the cells bear thread-like setae. Cells sol-
itary or in plate-like or branching colonies. Both zoospores
and gametes formed.   Family COLEOCHAETACEAE**

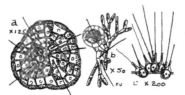

Figure 45

Fig.45. a, Coleochaete scutata
 Breb.; b, Coleochaete pulvinata
 Br.; c, Chaetosphaeridium sp.

Commonly found attached to higher
aquatic plants or to other algae.

**44a Zoospores and gametes produced in any vegetative cell and
never in specialized cells. The ends of branches are often
prolonged into colorless setae.   Family CHAETOPHORACEAE**

24

Figure 46

Fig.46. a, <u>Draparnaldia plumosa</u> Agar.; b, <u>Stigeoclonium lubricum</u> Katz.

Clear cool running water is its favorite habitat. The abundant branching is characteristic.

44b Zoospores and gametes produced in specialized cells, differing from vegetative cells. Chloroplasts often several in one cell. Family TRENTEPOHLIACEAE

Figure 47

Fig.47. <u>Ctenocladus circinnatus</u> Borzi.

The species of this family are less abundant than other members of the order.

ORDER CLADOPHORALES

45a Cells very long, 12 to 50 times their width. Chloroplasts numerous, in transverse bands. Gravel pits and flooded areas are said to be good places to look for it. Family SPHAEROPLEACEAE

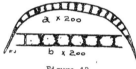

Figure 48

Fig.48. <u>Sphaeroplea annulina</u> Ag.; a, single celled young plant; b, part of one cell of filament.

45b Cells shorter, seldom with length more than eight times the width. Chloroplasts not in transverse band. Family CLADOPHORACEAE

Figure 49

Fig.49. a, <u>Cladophora glomerata</u> Kutz.

This family has both fresh water and marine species and is world-wide in its distribution.

ORDER ZYGNEMATALES

46a Cells cylindrical, united in filaments. Reproduce by conjugation process in which protoplasts have no chance to escape to exterior. Family ZYGNEMATACEAE

25

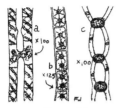

Figure 50

Fig.50. a, <u>Spirogyra</u> sp.; b, <u>Zygnema</u> sp.;
c, <u>Mougeotia</u> sp.

No one can get very far in nature lore
without hearing about Spirogyra. There are
many species, some with but one spiral chloroplast to the cell, others with several inter-
twined.

46b Cells of various shapes, usually solitary or occasionally
united into simple filaments. Figs. 51 and 52 47

47a Cell walls with vertical pores. In conjugation the protoplast escapes from the surrounding walls.
Family DESMIDIACEAE

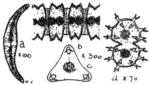

Figure 51

Fig.51. a, <u>Closterium</u> sp.; <u>Desmidium</u>
sp.; b, side view, c, end view;
d, <u>Schizocanthum</u> sp.

These highly interesting plants
somewhat resemble diatoms but do not
have stiff walls.

47b Cell walls without pores. The protoplast confined by walls
in conjugation. Family MESOTAENIACEAE

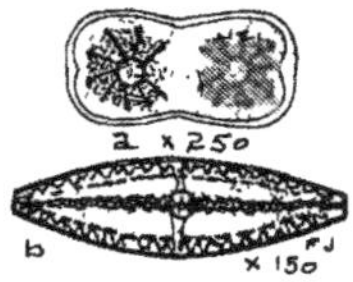

Figure 52

Fig.52. a, <u>Cylindrocystis diplospora</u> Lund.
Grows on damp soil; b, <u>Netrium digitus</u> I.& R.

A free-floating fresh-water species.

48a Plants yellow, yellowish-green or golden-brown. Mostly
microscopic species. Figs. 53 to 83 49

48b Plants brown or greenish-brown. Usually large plants, some
very large. Most species marine. Male gametes pear-shaped
with two flagella on the side. Figs. 84 to 100. (The Brown
Algae) 75

48c Plants red or purplish-green. Usually medium to large sized
plants. Most species marine. No motile reproductive cells.
Figs. 101 to 116. (The Red Algae) 86

49a Single celled plants (sometimes united in chains or circular
figures) with outer wall glass-like (of silica) and always composed of two overlapping parts (frustules) like a box and its
cover. Contents yellow or yellowish-brown. (The Diatoms).
Figs. 53 to 67 50

49b Not as in 49a. Figs. 68 to 83. 61

→ THE DIATOMS (BACILLARIEAE) ←

50a Frustules (outer walls) circular, polygonal or irregular in outline. Markings radiating from a center point. Figs. 53 to 56. 51

50b Frustules bilaterally symmetrical or irregular in surface view. Markings always arranged around a line and never around a point. Figs. 57 to 67 54

ORDER CENTRALES

51a Frustules without horns or prominent spines; shape a short cylinder. Most species disk-like though some are taller than broad.   Family COSCINODISCACEAE

Figure 53

Fig.53. a, Melosira varians Ag. grows in long filaments; b, Stephanodiscus niagarae Ehr. valve view, girdle view; c, Cyclotella meneghiniana Kutz.

"Frustule" seems to be about the best term for the entire wall or "shell" of a diatom. The word is sometimes used to include the contents, also.

51b Frustules with horns or prominent spines (some long cylindrical species lack spines or horns). Figs. 54 to 56. 52

52a Frustules elongated cylinders with many intercalary bands between the girdles.   Family RHIZOSOLENIACEAE

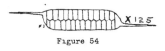

Figure 54

Fig.54. Rhizosolenia eriensis Smith.

"Valve" is used to refer to the face view or side of the frustule. The overlapping half on the wall is the hypotheca; while the smaller half is the epitheca.

52b Valves (face of frustule) with two or more thick horns or projections, the two families here-in treated are bilaterally symmetrical or asymmetrical but have the ornamentation radially arranged. Figs. 55 and 56. 53

53a Valves with spines or elevations at the angles.
                                            Family BIDDULPHIACEAE

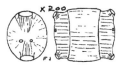

Figure 55

Fig.55. Biddulphia laevis Ehr.

A diatom so placed as to show the edges of the overlapping halves is said to present a girdle view.

53b Valves with internal partitions vertical to the valve face.
                                            Family ANAULACEAE

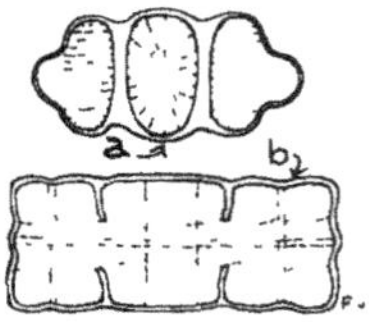

Figure 56

Fig.56. Terpsinoe americana Ralfs. a, valve
view; b, girdle view.

The very fine markings on the valves were
once much used to test microscopes.

ORDER PENNALES

54a The two valves always unlike, one having a raphe and the
other a pseudoraphe. There are no internal septa except in one
genus which has incomplete longitudinal ones.
                                         Family ACHNANTHACEAE

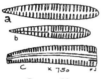

Figure 57

Fig.57. Rhoccosphenia curvata Grun.; a, outer
valve or epitheca; b, inner valve or hypotheca; c, girdle view.

Diatoms are world wide in their distribution.

54b Not as in 54a. Figs. 58 to 67. 55

55a The frustules usually elongate; the two valves alike in that
each has a raphe or each member of the pair has a pseudoraphe.
Figs. 58 to 62 56

55b Both valves with a true raphe which lies toward the middle
of the valve not in the marginal keel. Figs. 63 to 65 . . . 59

55c Both valves alike; each raphe somewhat concealed in a keel
at one or both sides of the valve. Figs. 66 and 67. 60

56a Valves bow-shaped, the raphe or pseudoraphe lying toward the
concave side. Girdle view rectangular or wedge-shaped.
                                          Family EUNOTIACEAE

Figure 58

Fig.58. a, Eunotia pectinalis Rab.;
b, Ceratoneis arcus Kutz.

A bit of slime from the bottom of any
watercourse is practically certain to be
filled with diatoms.

56b Not as in 56a. Figs. 59 to 62. 57

57a Valves wedge-shaped with transverse septa transversely
asymmetrical.   Family MERIDIONACEAE

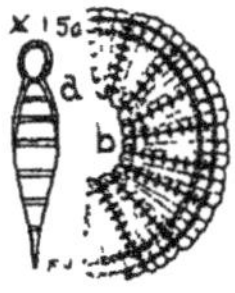

Figure 59

Fig.59. Meridion constrictum Ral.; a, valve view;
b, girdle view.

Many species of diatoms are known only as fossil
forms.

28

57b Not wedge-shaped. Figs. 60 to 62 58

58a With longitudinal internal septa (partitions). Valves transversely symmetrical; usually long.

Family TABELLARIACEAE

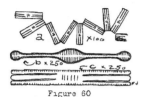

Figure 60

Fig.60. <u>Tabellaria</u> <u>fenestra</u> Kutz.; a, typical arrangement of colony; b, valve view; c, girdle view.

Immense deposits of the frustules of diatoms are found and have wide uses commercially. This is known as diatomaceous earth.

58b With transverse internal septa; symmetrical both transversely and longitudinally.

Family DIATOMACEAE

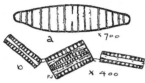

Figure 61

Fig.61. <u>Diatoma</u> <u>vulgari</u> Bory.; a, valve view; b, girdle view and typical colonial form.

Diatomaceous earth is used for polishing, as a filter in refining sugar, for heat insulation, to give body to dynamite, in brick and cementwork, and in many other ways.

58c With no internal septa. Both transversely and longitudinally symmetrical.

Family FRAGILARIACEAE

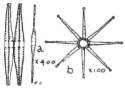

Figure 62

Fig.62. a, <u>Fragilaria</u> sp.; b, <u>Asterionella</u> <u>gracillima</u> Heib.

The free movement of diatoms in the water attracts attention. Of course, it must be remembered that the apparent speed is magnified the same as the size.

59a Valves symmetrical both transversely and longitudinally. Valves of many shapes.

Family NAVICULACEAE

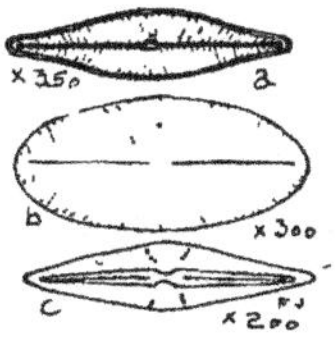

Figure 63

Fig.63. a, <u>Navicula</u> <u>rhyncocephala</u> Kutz.; b, <u>Diploneis</u> <u>elliptica</u> Cleve.; c, <u>Frustulia</u> <u>rhomboides</u> De T.

Streaming protoplasm seems to offer the best solution as to how a diatom propels itself.

59b Valves symmetrical longitudinally but not symmetrical transversely.

Family GOMPHONEMATACEAE

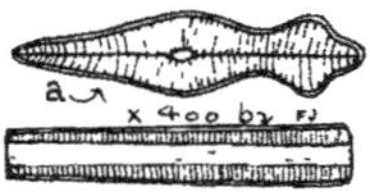

Figure 64

Fig.64. Gomphonema acuminatum Ehr.; a, valve
view; b, girdle view, a rather common fresh-
water form.

Reproduction of diatoms is most commonly by
cell division. Each half takes one valve and
grows a new wall for the other side.

59c Valves symmetrical transversely but not so longitudinally.
                                          Family CYMBELLACEAE

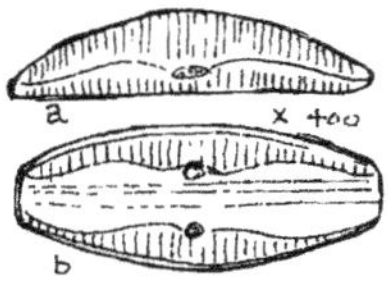

Figure 65

Fig.65. Amphora ovalis Kutz.; a, valve view;
b, girdle view.

This species is unusually large. The family
is a large one, too. Since the newly formed
wall part fits inside the old half, some of the
young diatoms are smaller than their parents
were.

60a With a single eccentric keel lying near one lateral margin.
                                          Family NITZSCHIACEAE

Figure 66

Fig.66. Hantzshia sp.

Two diatoms sometimes shed their outer
shells and fuse to later separate and grow
new shells. This is conjugation.

60b With two keels, one near each margin of the valve.
                                          Family SURIRELLACEAE

Figure 67

Fig.67. Surirella splendida Kutz.

Cell division of diatoms most usually takes place around midnight.

**61a Motile cells with flagella inserted in a transverse furrow;
one flagellum wraps around the cell transversely; the other
extends vertically backward. Contents of organism golden-brown
or colorless. Figs. 68 to 71. . . . . 63**

61b Plants without a transverse groove. Figs. 72 to 83 . . . 62

**62a Motile cells with two unequal flagella at anterior end.
Discoid chromatophores yellowish-green; without pyrenoids;
stored food, oil, not starch. The cell walls of many species
are made of H-shaped pieces which overlap. Figs. 72 to 79 . . 66**

**62b Motile cells with one or two flagella at the anterior end;
when two they may be either equal or unequal in length. Chromatophores are a distinctive golden-brown. Figs. 80 to 83 . . 71**

CLASS DINOPHYCEAE

This group of animal-like plants or plant-like animals (zoologists and botanists both claim them) are numerous--some 1000 species have been described but many points concerning their classification seems to be still questioned. They are likely of much less importance than other plants that have been omitted but some proposed orders are given.

**63a Motile, free swimming in vegetative state. Figs. 69 to
   71 . . . . 64**

**63b Vegetative stage non-motile*, free-floating or attached
   single celled. Reproduce only by zoospores or autospores.
                                         Order DINOCOCCALES**

Figure 68

Fig.68. Tetradinium minus Pash. a, mature
    vegetative plant; b, zoospore.

We have divided this class only to orders since there is still a great deal to learn about it before its classification is certain.

**64a Cell enclosed in a hard wall composed of a definite number
   of plates. Figs. 70 and 71. . . . . 65**

**64b Cell naked or if within a wall it is not divided into
   plates. Mostly solitary; a few colonial; mostly marine.
                                         Order GYMNODINIALES**

Figure 69

×200   Fig.69. a, Gymnodinium fascum Ehr. A fresh-water
           species.

**65a Wall divided vertically into two opposite halves (each with
   a definite number of plates). Known species all marine.
                                         Order DINOPHYSIDALES**

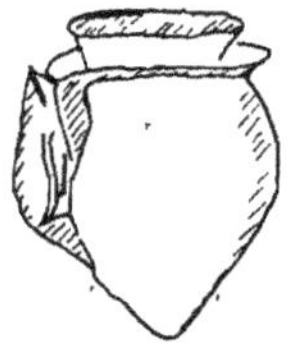

Figure 70

Fig.70. Dianophysis sp.

**65b Wall not separated vertically into two halves but divided
   into a definite number of plates. Wholly marine.
                                         Order PERIDINIALES**

---

*The non-motile Dinophyceae have been divided into four orders but since three of these have but one or two known species, they are not included in the key.

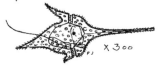

Figure 71

Fig.71. <u>Ceratium hirundinella</u> Sch.

CLASS HETEROKONTAE

66a Plant single celled with bulb-like multinucleate head and branching root-like parts, growing in soil.
Order HETEROSIPHONALES
Family BOTRYDIACEAE

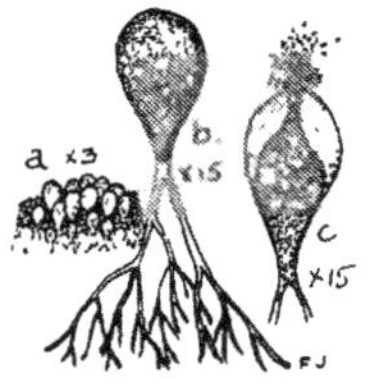

Figure 72

Fig.72. <u>Botrydium granulatum</u> Grev.; a, group of plants; b, single plant; c, zoospores being discharged from above-ground part.

These very interesting little plants are often common on the smooth ground of gardens and paths.

66b Cells arranged in filaments, either simple or branched. Figs. 77 to 83 70

66c Not like either 66a or 66b. Usually single celled. Surrounded by a wall. Figs. 73 to 76 67

ORDER HETEROCOCCALES

67a Cells always solitary. Figs. 75 and 76 69

67b Cells colonial or solitary. Figs. 73 and 74. 68

68a Cells cylindrical often in dendroid colonies; free-floating or epiphytic.
Family OPHIOCYTIACEAE

Figure 73

Fig.73. a, <u>Ophiocytium</u> spp.

Found in plankton and in pools.

68b Various shapes other than cylindrical; but one nucleus; cells small with one or a few chromatophores; reproduce only by autospores.
Family BOTRYOCOCCACEAE

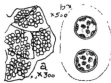

Figure 74

Fig.74. a, <u>Botryococcus braunii</u> Kutz.
b, <u>Chlorobotrys regularis</u> Boh.
Found in the plankton of clear-water lakes.

69a Cells usually with but one nucleus; large and with many chromatophores. Reproduce by both zoospores and autospores.

Family HALOSPHAERACEAE

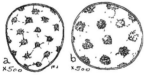

Fig.75. a, <u>Leuvenia natans</u> Gard. Grows in the film covering water.; b, <u>Botrydiopsis arhiza</u> Borzi. Grows on the surface of the ground.

Figure 75

69b Attached epiphytic forms often multinucleate with one to several chromatophores.   Family CHLOROTHECIACEAE

Fig.76. a, <u>Characiopsis pyriformis</u> Bor.; b, <u>Peroniella planctonica</u> Smith.

Many of the species of algae have but little apparent relation to man and his schemes.

Figure 76

ORDER HETEROTRICHALES

70a Filaments branched and multicellular.

Family MONOCILIACEAE

Fig.77. <u>Monocilia viridis</u> Gern.

The plants of this family are soil-growing species, some being found even at a depth of a few feet.

Figure 77

70b Filaments unbranched. No starch grains.

Family TRIBONEMATACEAE

Fig.78. <u>Tribonema</u> spp.; a, living plant; b, cell wall.

This family is very common in stagnant water. In early spring it is particularly abundant.

Figure 78

CLASS CHRYSOPHYCEAE

71a Cells motile during entire vegetative state or if amoeboid such condition is temporary. Figs. 80 to 83 72

71b Vegetative cells always non-motile and united in gelatinous colonies.

ORDER CHRYSOCAPSALES

Very much branched colonies in which cell division occurs only near the apices.   Family HYDRURACEAE

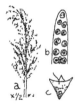

Figure 79

Fig.79. Hydrura foetidus Kir.; a, branch of
thallus; b, tip of thallus; c, zoospore.

Common on rocky bottoms of cold mountain streams.
As the species name suggests, it reveals itself by
its bad odor.

ORDER CHRYSOMONADALES

Figure 80

**72a But one apical flagellum present; ornamented
with scales and long spines.**
Family MALLOMONADACEAE

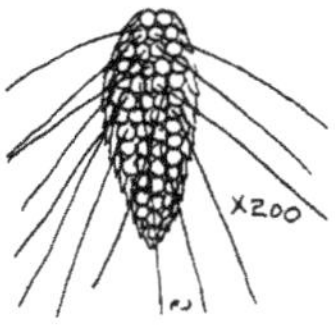

Fig.80. Mallomonas sp.

These plants are found in the floating growth
of our fresh-water lakes.

72b With 2 apical flagella. Figs. 81 to 83 73

73a Flagella of equal length. Figs. 82 and 83. 74

**73b Flagella unequal in length. Outer surface the same through-
out.**
Family OCHROMONADACEAE

Figure 81

Fig.81. a, Urognelopsis americana
Lemm. Very common in reservoirs and
lakes. Colonies may contain a
thousand cells.; b, Dinobryon sertu-
laria Ehr.; colony and individuals.

This species and other members of
the genus are common in the plankton of
fresh-water lakes.

74a Outer surface of the cells interrupted with scales of silica.
Family SYNURACEAE

Figure 82

Fig.82. Synura uvella Ehr.

Inhabits the plankton of lakes and smaller
bodies of water.

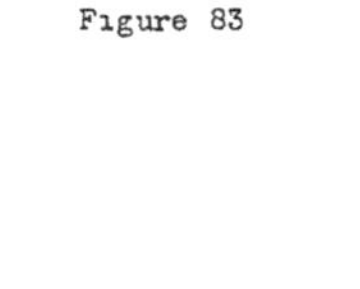

74b Outer surface of cells the same throughout.
Family SYNCRYPTACEAE

Figure 83

Fig.83. Syncrypta volvox Ehr.

Many of the motile algae have a red eyespot
but this species is not thus equipped.

THE BROWN ALGAE (PHAEOPHYTA)

CLASS ISOGENERATAE

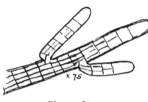

77a Greater part of thallus with tiers of
elongated vertical cells. Thallus with
one large apical cell at tip from which
all growth starts.

Family SPHACELARIACEAE

Figure 84

Fig.84. Sphacelaria californica Sauv.

Members of this family are marine and
constitute much of the food of some plant-
eating fish and other marine animals.

77b. Thallus filamentous and branched; usually but one cell in
diameter. Reproduce by zoospores and isogametes.

Family ECTOCARPACEAE

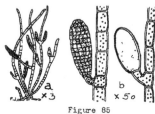

Fig.85. Ectocarpus cylindricus Saund.;
a, portion of plant; b, a gametangium; c, a sporangium.

These plants are usually attached
to coarser algae. They are marine. .

Figure 85

77c Upper part of thallus usually one cell in diameter; lower
part with elongated cells in transverse tiers.

Family TILOPTERIDACEAE

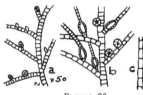

Fig.86. Haplospora globosa Kjel.;
a, upper part of sporophyte; b, upper part of gametophyte; c, lower
part of thallus.

Figure 86

Figure 87

78a Alternating generations differ widely in size and form; asexual plants often disk-like.   Family CUTLERIACEAE

Fig.87. Cutleria multifida; a, sexual plant; b, young asexual plant.

It is found in the warmer parts of the north Atlantic.

78b Alternating generations quite similar in general appearance.
Family DICTYOTACEAE

Figure 88

Fig.88. Dictyota dichotoma Lam.; a, female plant; b, male plant; c, asexual plant. (The reproductive organs are enlarged out of proportion to the thalli in the drawing.)

One investigator reports a fair sized plant of this species which produced over 500 million sperms at one time. Many of nature's creatures are thus highly prolific.

CLASS HETEROGENERATAE

79a Thallus built of thread-like branching filaments often attached to each other at their base. Figs. 89 to 92. 80

79b A thallus with true parenchymatous tissue is formed by intercalary longitudinal division. Figs. 93 to 98 82

80a A larger sporophyte of sporangia bearing branching filaments alternates with a microscopic monoecious gametophyte which reproduces by isogametes. Figs. 91 and 92 81

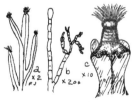

Figure 89

80b Sporophyte with each tip terminating in a tuft of hairs. Microscopic monoecious gametophyte reproduces by sperms and eggs.   Order SPOROCHNALES
Family SPOROCHNACEAE

Fig.89. Carpomitra cabrerae Kutz.; a, part of sporophyte; b, gametophyte; c, enlarged tip of sporophyte.

80c Each sporophyte ending in a single filament. The microscopic gametophyte produces sperms and eggs.   Order DESMARESTIALES
Family DESMARESTIACEAE

Figure 90

Fig.90. Desmarestia herbacea Lamx.; a, portion of thallus; b, female gametophyte; c, male gametophyte.

The sporophyte attains a length of several feet. Rather common along the Pacific coast.

36

ORDER CHORDARIALES

81a Sporophyte erect cylindrical single or branched. Gameto-phyte filamentous; microscopic. Family CHORDARIACEAE

Fig.91. <u>Mesogloia vermiculata</u> Le J.;
a, sporophyte; b, gametophyte.

This plant belongs to the north Atlantic.

Figure 91

81b Sporophyte spreading over surface of attachment. Globular, solid or hollow. Family LEATHESIACEAE

Fig.92. <u>Leathesia difformis</u> Aresc.;
a, sporophyte; b, sporangia;
c, gametophyte.

A northern species found in both the Atlantic and Pacific oceans.

Figure 92

82a Sporophyte of medium size, parenchymatous tissue all much the same; grows by intercalary cell division; gametophyte microscopic. Figs. 93 to 95. 83

82b Sporophyte with definite holdfast, stipe and blade; often very large. Growth due to intercalary meristem. Gametophyte microscopic and producing sperms and eggs. (The Kelps) In this order are found the largest algae known. Figs. 96 to 98 84

82c Thallus cylindrical, much branched; new growth from a single apical cell. Gametophyte microscopic; produces isogametes.
Order DICTYOSIPHONALES
Family DICTYOSIPHONACEAE

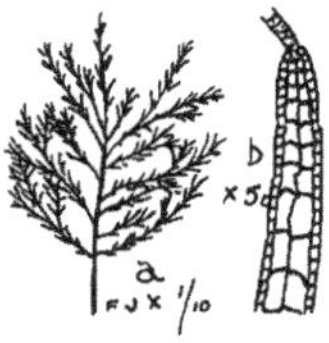

Fig.93. <u>Dictyosiphon foeniculaceus</u> Kutz.;
a, sporophyte; b, tip of branch.

Found on both the Atlantic and Pacific coasts.

Figure 93

ORDER PUNCTARIALES

83a Apparently only the gametophyte known; hairs in groups; gametangia palisade-like not reaching beyond the surface.
Family SCYTOSIPHONACEAE

37

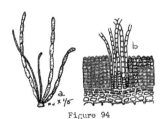

Figure 94

Fig.94. Scytosiphon lomentaria Agar.; a, part of gametophyte; b, section through a gametangium.

Widely scattered on all our coasts.

83b Both sporophyte and gametophyte small but macroscopic when mature; hairs present. Sporangia in elevated sori.
Family ASPEROCOCCACEAE

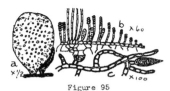

Figure 95

Fig.95. Soranthera ulvoidea P.& R.; a, sporophyte covered with sori; b, section through sorus; c, game- tophyte.

Common along the Pacific coast.

ORDER LAMINARIALES

84a Sporophyte simple, with unbranched stipe; the lamina some- times cut or divided. Holdfast often branched, sometimes disk- like.
Family LAMINARIACEAE

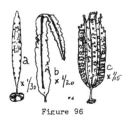

Figure 96

Fig.96. a, Laminaria saccharina Lam.; b, Cymathaere triplicata Ag.; c, Costaria costata Saund.

The family is a large one and some of the species attain considerable size. It has importance as a food source in Japan.

84b Sporophyte simple or irregularly branched. Sori almost com- pletely covers both sides of lamina.
Family ALARIACEAE

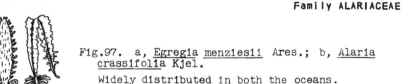

Figure 97

Fig.97. a, Egregia menziesii Ares.; b, Alaria crassifolia Kjel.

Widely distributed in both the oceans.

84c Sporophyte more or less compound with stipe divided or branching and few to many lamina. **Family LESSONIACEAE**

38

Figure 98

Fig.98. a, <u>Macrocystis</u> <u>pyrifera</u> Ag.
This very common west coast spe-
cies may attain a length of 175
feet; b, <u>Postelsia</u> <u>palmaeformis</u>
Rupr.

This so called sea-palm though
only 15 to 20 inches high attracts
much interest by its tree-like appearance.

ORDER FUCALES

**85a Thallus flattened with all branching in one plane. Female
gametangium producing 8-4-2-1 large viable eggs.**

Family FUCACEAE

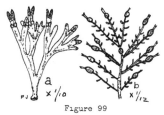

Figure 99

Fig.99. a, <u>Fucus</u> <u>vesiculosus</u> L.;
b, <u>Ascophyllum</u> <u>nodosum</u> Le J.

This is a standard laboratory
plant. It has some other uses also
such as being a source of iodine.

**85b Thallus rounded and branching from all sides, female game-
tangium producing but one large viable egg.**

Family SARGASSACEAE

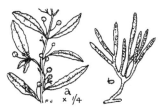

Figure 100

Fig.100. a, <u>Sargassum</u> sp.; b, <u>Pycnophy-
cus</u> <u>tuberculatus</u> Kutz.

Some 150 species of Sargassum have
been named. It is a familiar sight
along the beach of the Gulf of Mexico
and other warm waters where its plants
are washed up on the shores.

THE RED ALGAE (RHODOPHYTA)

**86a Thallus enlarges by intercalary growth; zygote divides di-
rectly into carpospores. A few species are unicellular.**

Order BANGIALES
Family BANGIACEAE

Figure 101

Fig.101. a, <u>Porphyra</u> <u>perforata</u> Ag. Common along
both our coasts; b, <u>Porphyridium</u> <u>cruentum</u> Nag.
Appears as a red crust on damp earth.

86b Thallus grows only at tip; carpospores arise indirectly from
the zygote. Figs. 102 to 116. 87

87a Sporophyte generation represented only the zygote. Male and
female gametophytes well developed. Figs. 104 to 107. . . . 91

87b A definite sporophyte generation alternating with male and
female gametophytes. Figs. 102, 103 and 108 to 116. 88

88a Without an auxiliary cell (separate vegetative cell which
receives the zygote nucleus in its migration from the carpo-
gonium); the sporophyte developing directly from the carpo-
gonium.   Family GELIDIACEAE

Fig.102. Gelidium corneum Lam.
It is the members of this family that furnish
agar-agar, the most valuable product coming from any
of the algae.

Figure 102

88b Auxiliary cell present. Figs. 103 and 108 to 116 89

89a Auxiliary cell arising on a special filament. Figs. 108
to 110 92

89b Not as in 88a. Figs. 103 and 111 to 116. 90

90a Auxiliary cell arising from a vegetative cell of the gametophyte. Figs. 111 to 113 94

90b Auxiliary cell a special cell prepared before fertilization.
                                         Order RHODYMENIALES

Carpogonial branch three celled.   Family RHODYMENIACEAE

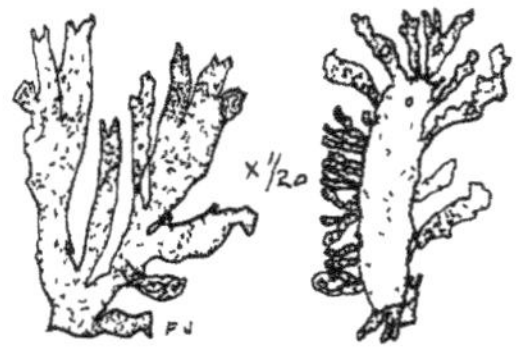

Fig.103. Rhodymenia palmata Grev.
This plant is an article of food in
some regions and is sometimes used for
chewing, like tobacco.

Figure 103

90c A special auxiliary cell prepared after fertilization.
Figs. 114 to 116 95

ORDER NEMALIONALES

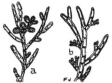

Figure 104

91a   Thallus without central axis and without whorls of branches.   Family CHANTRANSIACEAE

Fig.104.   <u>Acrochaetium</u> <u>rhipidandrum</u> Kyl.;
a, female gametophyte; b, male gametophyte.

Figure 105

91b   Thallus with a main axis surrounded by thick whorled tufts of finer filaments. Family BATRACHOSPERMACEAE

Fig.105.   <u>Batrachospermum</u> <u>moniliforme</u> Roth.;
a, part of plant; b, whorls and reproductive organs.

This is a fresh water species.

91c   Thallus of branching filaments for most part only one cell in diameter.   The zygote grows an uncovered tuft of surrounding filaments.   Family HELMINTHOCLADIACEAE

Figure 106

Fig.106.   <u>Nemalion</u> <u>miltifidum</u> Ag.;
a, vegetative plant; b, reproductive organs, 1, male, 2, female; c and d, early and later stages of spore formation.

91d   Thallus of slender colorless filaments dichotomously branched Carposporophyte surrounded by a pericarp.
Family CHAETANGIACEAE

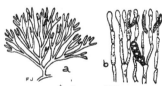

Figure 107

Fig.107.   <u>Scinaia</u> <u>furcellata</u> Biv.;
a, part of thallus; b, cells within filament.

This species is found in the Atlantic and Mediterranean.

ORDER CRYPTONEMIALES

92a   Plants much incrusted with lime; antheridia in conceptacles with a pore outlet.   Family CORALLINACEAE

Figure 108

Fig.108.   a, <u>Lithothamnion</u> sp.
b, <u>Corallina</u> <u>mediterranea</u>.

Members of this family are often so encrusted and stiff as to appear coral like, hence the name.

41

92b Not incrusted with lime 93

93a Thallus grows only at terminal cells; no procarp. Carpo-
gonium and auxiliary cells on special multicellular branches.
Family DUMONTIACEAE

Figure 109

Fig.109. _Dudresnaya purpurifera_ Ag.; part of plant.
Reproduction in the red algae is usually a com-
plicated process.

93b Carpogonial branches and the auxiliary cell branches
gathered into bodies on the surface of the thallus.
Family SQUAMARIACEAE

Figure 110

Fig.110. _Peyssonnelia squamaria_ Dec.
These plants are sometimes encrusted
with lime.

ORDER GIGARTINALES

94a Basal cell becomes the auxiliary cell. Thallus fleshy,
dichotomously branched.   Family GIGARTINACEAE

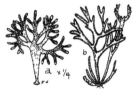

Figure 111

Fig.111. a, _Chondrus crispus_ Stac.;
b, _Gigartina_ sp.
The first named species, known as
Irish Moss is much used for several food
dishes.

94b A daughter cell of the basal cell becomes the auxiliary
cell, appearing after fertilization.
Family RHODOPHYLLIDACEAE

Figure 112

Fig.112. _Cystoclonium purpurascens_ Kutz.;
a, part of frond; b, auxiliary cell and
goniomoblast.

94c Auxiliary cell large, surrounded by several carpogonial
cells. Many nutritive cells present.   Family RISSOELLACEAE

Figure 113

Fig.113. _Rissoella verruculosa_ Ag.; a, frond; b, cross section showing auxiliary cell.

ORDER CERAMIALES

95a Thallus leafy, sometimes with a midrib.

Family DELESSERIACEAE

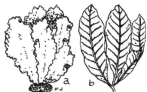

Figure 114

Fig.114. a, _Grinnellia americana_ Har.; b, _Delesseria sanguinea._

Many of the most beautiful of the red algae belong in this rather large family.

95b Thallus of branched filaments. Figs. 115 and 116. 96

96a Filaments monosiphonous (but one cell in diameter).

Family CERAMIACEAE

Figure 115

Fig.115. _Callithamnion corymbosum_ Lyn.; branch of tetrasporic generation.

96b Filaments polysiphonous (more than one cell in diameter).

Family RHODOMELACEAE

Figure 116

Fig.116. a, _Dasya elegans_ Ag.; b, _Polysiphonia violaceae_ Har.

These fine-cut plants are very attractive, especially when floating in water.

43

⇥ THE LICHENS (Phylum Lichenes) ⇤

The situation here is different from all other parts of the plant kingdom. Technically the Lichens are not in themselves individual plants but plant corporations or partnerships, the individual members of which already have places elsewhere in the families of fungi and algae. The keys that follow consider these plants, then,as corporate bodies and not the individual components. Some botanists prefer to thus give the Lichens a place of their own in the classification. Others wish to distribute them among the fungi and algae to which their component symbionts belong. Those of such mind may disregard these keys.

1a Lichens in which the spores are borne on basidia (clubs). They take the form of bracket fungi. Order BASIDIOLICHENES

This order including but a limited number of tropical species, no further division of them will be attempted.

1b Lichens which bear their spores in sacs (asci). Figs. 117 to 126. 2

ORDER ASCOLICHENES

2a Closely growing scale-like (crustose) lichens (some parasitic species) with very minute projecting fruiting bodies (stipe) which are usually not branched. Algal symbiont, Chlorococcum. Family CALICIACEAE

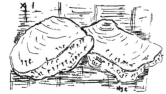

Figure 117

Fig.117. Calicium polyporaeum Nyl.

Grows parasitically on bracket fungi. The thallus so blends with its host as to be almost indistinguishable.

2b Apothecia elongate and often branched. Algal symbiont usually Trentepohlia (Family Chlorophyceae) Thallus crustose. Family GRAPHIDACEAE

Figure 118

Fig.118. Graphis scripta Ach.

Thallus smooth, thin, ashy or olive on bark of trees. Apothecia 1/8 inch or more in length.

2c Apothecia disk or cup-shaped (a few with nearly closed fruiting bodies). Thallus of many forms. Figs. 120 to 126 3

2d Apothecia surrounded by a perithecium leaving only an ostiole at apex. Symbiont <u>Trentepohlia</u> or <u>Protococcus</u>. Thallus foliose.

Family DERMATOCARPACEAE

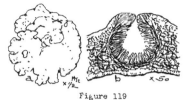

Figure 119

Fig.119. <u>Dermatocarpon miniatum</u> Fr. a, typical thallus; b, section through fruiting body.

Usually found on limestone. It is very widely distributed.

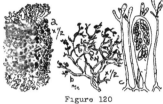

Figure 120

3a Thallus and apothecia deep yellow or orange; form variable.

Family TELOSCHISTACEAE

Fig.120. a, <u>Placodium elegans</u> Ach.; <u>Telochristes chrysopthalmus</u> Fr. b, part of thallus; c, ascus and paraphyses.

3b Not deep yellow or orange. Figs. 121 to 126 4

4a With prominent erect fruiting bodies sometimes branched and often brightly colored. Figs. 122 and 123. 5

4b Main part of plant a leaflike thallus. Figs. 124 to 126 . 6

4c Main part of plant crustose. Apothecia rounded.

Family LECIDEACEAE

Figure 121

Fig.121. <u>Buellia myriocarpa</u> Mudd., a, typical plant; b, section through fruiting body; c, ascus.

This is a large family with many widely distributed species.

5a With basal vegetative part and erect fruiting bodies (podetia) simple or somewhat branched. Fruiting bodies often scarlet or brown with concave or convex hymenia.

Family CLADONIACEAE

Figure 122

Fig.122. a, <u>Cladonia rangiferina</u> Web., Reindeer Moss. A beautiful ashy-gray plant often growing in great abundance over earth and rocks. Widely distributed. b, <u>Cladonia pyxidata</u> Hoff.

On earth and rotten wood; cosmopolitan.

5b   Basal thallus disappearing before maturity. Apothecia at ends of much branched fruiting bodies.

Family STEREOCAULACEAE

Fig.123. <u>Stereocaulon coralloides</u> Fr.; a, typical plant; b, tip of branch showing small disk-like apothecia.

Figure 123

6a   Thallus rather closely attached to supporting body so as to be only sub-foliose, or some what crustose. The algal symbiont usually one of the Chlorococcaceae.   Family LECANORACEAE

Fig.124. <u>Lecanora subfusca</u> Ach.; a, thallus with apothecia; b, section through apothecium.

Common on trees and sometimes on rock. Light green to whitish with fruiting cups almost black.

Figure 124

6b   Plants with large foliose parts; apothecia usually buried In the lobes of the thallus, sometimes on under side.

Family PELTIGERACEAE

Fig.125. <u>Peltigera aphthosa</u> Willd.

On earth and rocks. Scattered throughout much of the northern hemisphere. Above apple-green to brownish, below white when fresh, often with veins dark. Sometimes mistaken for a liverwort.

Figure 125

6c   Thallus plainly foliose or sometimes fruticose.

Family PARMELIACEAE

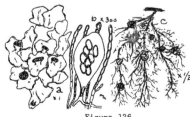

Fig.126. <u>Parmelia perlata</u> Ach.; a, typical plant; b, ascus and paraphyses.

Common on rocks; widely scattered.

c, <u>Usnea barbata</u> Fr., a hanging form which roughly resembles "Spanish Moss".

Figure 126

```
┌──────────────────────┐
│   KEY TO THE FAMILIES │
│     OF THE FUNGI      │
└──────────────────────┘
```

1a   Vegetative body, a plasmodium (naked slimy mass of living
      substance flowing in decaying wood, leaves, etc., usually in
      the dark). Reproductive bodies, tiny knob or plume-like struc-
      tures (sporangia) usually in groups and of various colors.
      Figs. 138 to 144. (The Slime Molds) 15

1b   Not as in 1a. 2

2a   Microscopic single celled plants (often clinging in groups
      or chains). Reproduction by dividing through middle (fission).
      Figs. 127 to 137. (The Bacteria). 3

2b   Fungi with vegetative body of filaments and various repro-
      ductive organs. Figs. 145 to 200. (The True Fungi) 21

```
┌──────────────────────────────────────┐
│   THE BACTERIA (SCHIZOMYCETES)        │
└──────────────────────────────────────┘
```

3a   Cells living only parasitically within the cells of animals.
                                           Order RICKETTSIALES
                                           Family RICKETTSIACEAE

      Dermocentroxenus rickettsii, Rocky Mountain Spotted Fever.

      It is transmitted by the bite of some species of ticks
      which in turn have gotten the organism from some of the rodents
      which serve as reservoirs for the disease. The disease is now
      also found in regions other than the Rocky Mountains. No draw-
      ing has been attempted since there is so little one can picture
      for some of the smallest bacteria.

3b   Cells capable of living other than as parasites within the
      cells of animals 4

4a   Cells self sustaining by oxidation of sulphur or by photo-
      synthesis through green or purple pigments. Plant-like spores
      rarely if ever found. The Sulphur Bacteria.
                                           Order THIOBACTERIALES

      Cells containing bacteriopurpurin, and sometimes sulfur
      granules. Cells of various shapes but not filamentous.
                                           Family RHODOBACTERIACEAE

      The species of this rather large family may be spherical or
      rod shaped and single cells or in colonies. The red or purple
      color is characteristic. No picture has been attempted since
      the color is the most distinguishing factor.

4b   Cells not as in 4a. 5

5a   Cells attached by a gelatinous base or with a gelatinous
      stalk. The Stalked Bacteria.
                                           Order CAULOBACTERIALES

      With stalks of ferric hydroxide.
                                           Family GALLIONELLACEAE

47

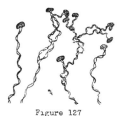

Figure 127

Fig.127. <u>Gallionella</u> <u>ferruginea</u>.

The attaching bands are ribbon-like and much twisted.

5b   Cells without a gelatinous stalk or base. Figs. 128 to 137. 6

6a   Cells collecting into masses and forming cysts or fruiting bodies. The Slime Bacteria.   Order MYXOBACTERIALES

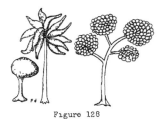

Figure 128

Apparently not very well known. One family of course would be
                          MYXOBACTERIACEAE

Fig.128. Fruiting bodies of three species of this order.

These plants in some ways, of course, resemble the Slime Molds.

6b   Cells not as in 6a. Figs. 129 to 137 7

7a   Very slender spiral rods, motile but without apparent flagella. Protozoa-like.   Order SPIROCHAETALES
                          Family SPIROCHAETACEAE

Figure 129

Fig.129. a, <u>Treponema</u> <u>pallidum</u>. This organism is the causative agent of syphilis in man. b, <u>Spirochaete</u> <u>plicatelis</u>; c, <u>Spirochaete</u> <u>obermeieri</u>.

The spirochetes are slimmer than the members of the genus <u>Spirillum</u> and are more like the protozoa.

7b   Cells not as in 7a. Figs. 130 to 137 8

8a   Cells (usually filamentous) covered with a gelatinous sheath which is often encrusted with an iron compound. The Sheathed or Iron Bacteria.   Order CHLAMYDOBACTERIALES
                          Family CHLAMYDOBACTERIACEAE

Figure 130

Fig.130. a, <u>Crenothrix</u> <u>polyspora</u>; b, <u>Leptothrix</u> <u>hyalina</u>.

These are apparently forms between the true bacteria and the simplest algae and protozoans. They are known as "Higher bacteria" or <u>Trichobacteria</u>.

48

LOWER BACTERIA — FILTERABLE VIRUSES

At the other extreme are those organisms much smaller and still more simple than bacteria. They are ultra-microscopic; likely too small to be seen by the ordinary microscope. There is plenty of evidence, however, of their existence.

8b Cells not sheathed. Figs. 131 to 137 9

9a Cells often branched, usually elongated or filament-like and sometimes forming a mycelium. Figs. 136 and 137 14

9b Cells not forming a mycelium or branching and not especially elongate. The True Bacteria. Figs. 131 to 135. 10

ORDER EUBACTERIALES

10a Cells self sustaining by oxidizing a nitrite or ammonia.
Family NITROBACTERIACEAE

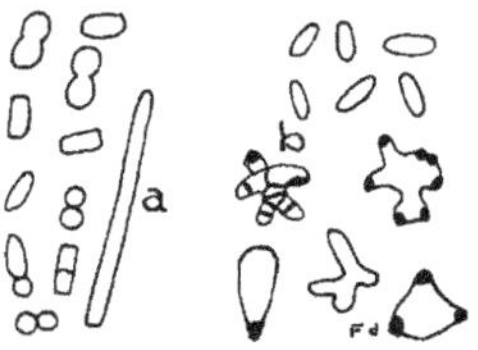

Figure 131

Fig.131. a, Acetobacter pasteurinum Beig.; b, Normal and involute forms of Rhizobium leguminosarum Frank.

They play an important part in the activities of soils and sewage disposal.

10b Cells not living on inorganic materials. Figs. 132 to 135. 11

Figure 132

11a Cells spherical in shape although often becoming oval before dividing.
Family COCCACEAE

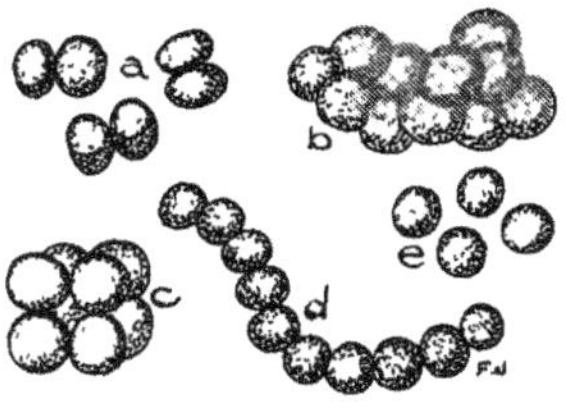

Fig.132. a, cells in pairs, Diplococcus; b, in irregular masses, Staphylococcus; c, in cubes, Sarcina; d, in chains, Streptococcus; e, cells scattered, Micrococcus.

11b Cells normally elongated; especially when in active growth. Figs. 133 to 135 12

12a Cells curved or spiral usually with flagella at the ends.
Family SPIRILLACEAE

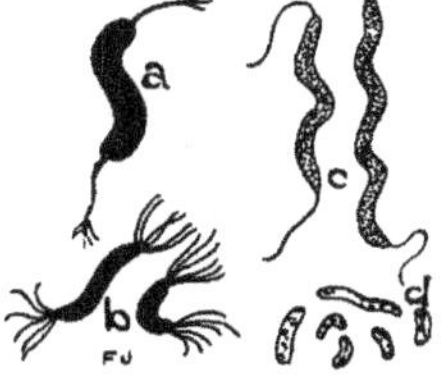

Figure 133

Fig.133. a, Spirillum undulata; b, Spirillum rubrum; c, Spirillum volutans; d, Vibrio cholerae.

In studying movement of bacteria the student should not confuse it with "Brownian movement", the trembling of minute objects when highly magnified. This is likely due to a molecular bombardment.

49

12b Cells straight or but slightly bent. Figs. 134 and 135. .13

13a Species producing spores within the cells (endospores).
Family BACILLACEAE

Figure 134

Fig.134. a, <u>Bacillus</u> <u>subtilis</u> Cohn.; b, <u>Bacillus</u> <u>cohaerens</u>; c, <u>Clostridium</u> <u>butyricum</u> Praz.

Spores offer a means of living through unfavorable times. These bacteria, then, are especially hard to kill.

13b Species not forming endospores.
Family BACTERIACEAE

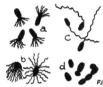

Figure 135

Fig.135. a, <u>Pseudomonas</u> <u>syncyanea</u>; b, <u>Proteus</u> <u>vulgaris</u>; c, <u>Pseudomonas</u> <u>macroselmis</u>; d, <u>Escherichia</u> <u>coli</u>.

Only part of the members of this family are motile. The family ranks at the top when considered from the economic viewpoint.

ORDER ACTINOMYCETALES

14a Filamentous and branching, often forming a mycelium. Family ACTINOMYCETACEAE

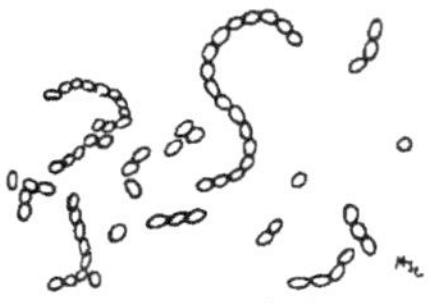

Fig.136. <u>Actinomyces</u> sp.

These bacteria resemble molds in their behavior. One species seems to be related to the cattle disease, lumpy jaw.

Figure 136

14b No mycelium and but rarely branched.
Family MYCOBACTERIACEAE

Figure 137

Fig.137. a, <u>Mycobacterium</u> <u>tuberculosis</u>. The causative agent of human tuberculosis; b, <u>Corynebacterium</u> <u>diphtheriae</u>.

The diptheria organism.

⇢ THE SLIME MOLDS (MYXOTHALLOPHYTA) ⇠

15a Species that live as parasites on other plants. (Body within tissue of host naked, multinucleate and usually not forming a wall even when spores develop.)
Order PLASMODIOPHORALES
Family PLASMODIOPHORACEAE

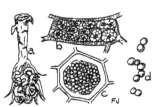

Figure 138

Fig.138. <u>Plasmodiophora</u> <u>brassicae</u>, Club-root of Cabbage. a, stem and root of diseased cabbage plant; b, cell of cabbage filled with amoeboid cells of the parasite; c, cell filled with spores; d, individual spores.

15b Species that are saprophytic. Figs. 139 to 144 16

16a Vegetative phase of free amoeba which gather in aggregations for fruiting. Found on dung of animals and in soil.

Order ACRASIALES
Family ACRASIACEAE

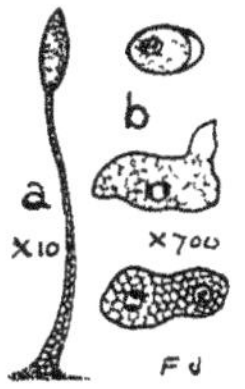

Fig.139. <u>Dictyostelium</u> sp.; a, fruiting body; b, individual cells.

Figure 139

16b Vegetative stage consisting of a mass of slime (plasmodium) which has many nuclei and a flowing movement. Figs. 140 to 144. 17

CLASS MYXOMYCETES

17a Spores borne internally within a sporangium. Fruiting bodies varying widely in shape and color and developing from a plasmodium which has lived within decaying logs, masses of decaying leaves, etc. A large majority of the slime molds belong here 18

17b Spores borne externally on erect fruiting growths.

Order EXOSPORALES
Family CERATIOMYXACEAE

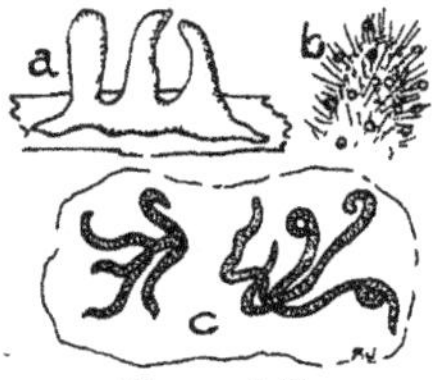

Fig.140. <u>Ceratiomyxa</u> <u>fruticulosa</u>; a, fruiting pillars; b, tip of a pillar enlarged; fruiting bodies of another species.

Figure 140

ORDER ENDOSPORALES

18a Sporangia with spores supported by a frame work of netted threads (capillitium). Figs. 141 to 144 19

18b With no capillitium or very poorly developed. Outer wall of sporangia (peridium) with thinner areas at top.

Family CRIBRARIACEAE

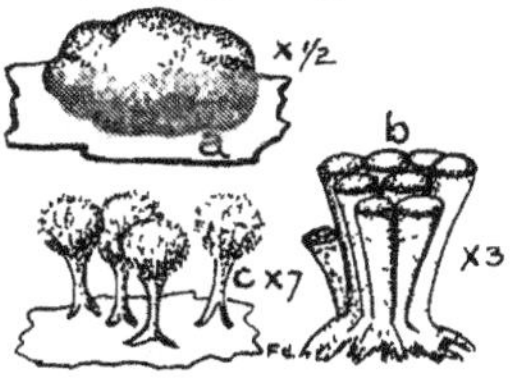

Fig.141. A <u>Enteridium</u> <u>splendens</u> Morg.; b, <u>Tribifera</u> <u>ferruginosa</u> Macb.; c, <u>Cribraria</u> <u>argillacea</u> Pers.

The perfection of these tiny fruiting bodies are a constant source of wonder to the thoughtful student.

Figure 141

51

19a Deposits of lime plainly evident throughout the fruiting body. Spores black.   Family PHYSARACEAE

Fig.142. a, <u>Diderma</u> <u>testaceum</u> Pers.; b, <u>Badhamia</u> <u>papaveraceae</u> B. R.; c, <u>Physarum</u> <u>viride</u> Dit.; d, <u>Fuligo</u> <u>septica</u> L.

One needs to see the delicate coloring of many slime molds to properly appreciate them.

Figure 142

19b Limy deposits absent (rarely scanty). Figs. 143 and 144 . 20

20a Sporangia (fruiting bodies) with a columella (central shaft) and many capillitium threads (frame work).
                                               Family STEMONITACEAE

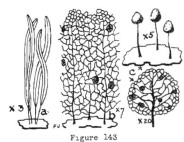

Fig.143. a, <u>Stemonitus</u> <u>morgani</u> Peck; b, <u>Stemonitus</u> <u>confluens</u> E. & C.; c, <u>Comatricha</u> <u>nigra</u> Pers.

<u>Stemonitus</u> resembles a group of tiny ostrich plumes.

Figure 143

20b Without columella; capillitium threads hollow and usually ornamented. Spores usually yellow, never black or purple.
                                               Family TRICHIACEAE

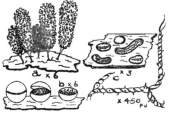

Fig.144. a, <u>Arcyria</u> <u>denudata</u> Pers.; b, <u>Perichaena</u> <u>corticalis</u> Rost.; c, <u>Trichia</u> <u>iowensis</u> Macb. and capillitium thread.

Figure 144

⇾ | THE HIGHER FUNGI (EUMYCETES) | ⇽

21a Vegetative branches (mycelium) continuous (having no cross walls) (aseptate). (The Algal-like Fungi). Figs. 145 to 158. 23

21b Mycelium with cross walls (septate) (all higher fungi with fruiting bodies one-half inch or more across, belong here). Figs. 159 to 200 22

22a Spores borne in sacks (asci). The Sac Fungi. Figs.
     159 to 185 36

22b Spores borne on clubs (basidia). The Club Fungi. Figs.
     186 to 200 60

⇥ | THE ALGAL-LIKE FUNGI (PHYCOMYCETES) | ⇤

23a Sexual reproduction by small spermatazoids and larger eggs
     (heterogamous). Sub-class OOMYCETES. Figs. 145 to 153 . . 24

23b Sexual reproduction by fusion of equal sized motile sex
     cells (isogamous). Sub-class ZYGOMYCETES. Figs. 154 to
     158. 32

24a Conidia present. Parasitic on other land plants. Figs.
     145 and 146. 25

24b No conidia; reproducing only by sexual spores and zoospores.
     Fig. 147 to 153. 26

ORDER PERONOSPORALES

25a Sporangiophores extending beyond the host tissue, usually
     branched; conidiospores not in chains.   Family PERONOSPORACEAE

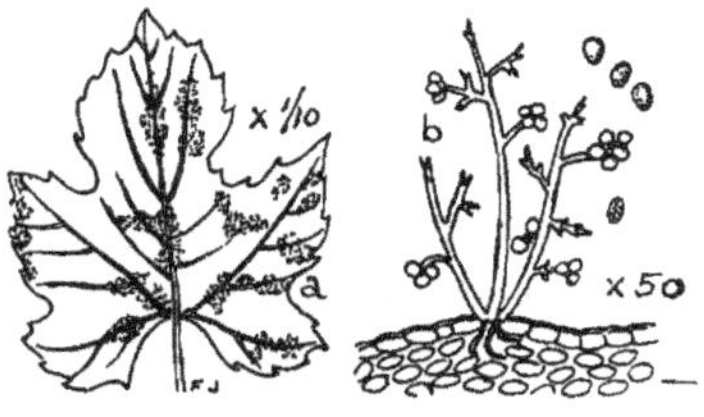

Figure 145

Fig.145. Plasmopara viticola
B.& D., Downy-mildew of Grapes;
a, Grape Leaf with patches of
downy mildew; b, conidiophores
and spores arising from tissue
of host.

Many disease producing-fungi are
included in these "downy mildews".

25b Sporangiophores forming under the epidermis of the host
     plant, unbranched; spores in chains.   Family ALBUGINACEAE

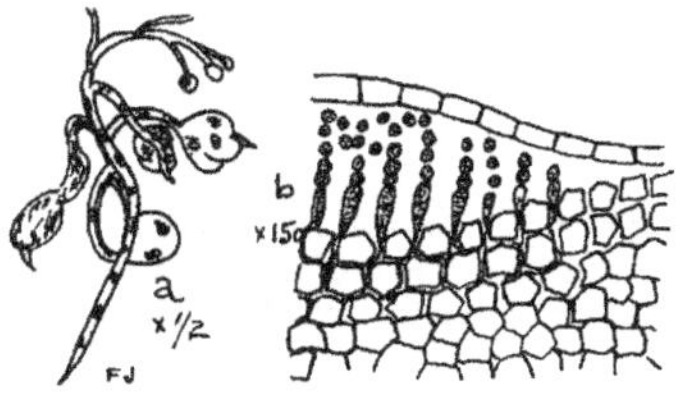

Figure 146

Fig.146. Albugo candida Kuntz.,
White Rust of Crucifers; a, de-
formed radish plant infected with
Albugo; b, Section showing growth
of conidia on host.

The white blister-like sori of
these plants give the name "white
rust". The diseased parts are de-
formed and swollen.

26a Plant filaments (mycelia) poorly developed; often only a
     single cell. Parasitic on other fungi, algae or seed bearing
     plants. Figs. 147 to 149. 27

26b Plant filaments of more than one cell though sometimes much
     reduced. Figs. 150 to 153 29

ORDER CHYTRIDALES

27a. Reproductive zoospores and gametes without flagella; a globular fertile part outside of host with thread-like vegetative parts extended inward. Family RHIZIDIACEAE

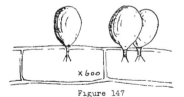

Figure 147

Fig.147. Rhizophidium ovatum Couch.

This like many other parasites makes a rapid growth, the life cycle in this case requiring less than one day.

27b Reproductive cells with one or more flagella; living wholly within the host. Figs. 148 and 149 28

28a All tissue fertile; confined to a single host cell. Family OLPIDIACEAE

Figure 148

Fig.148. Olpidium brassicae Dang.; a, resting spores; b, spores with single flagellum.

Some of these parasites have both summer and winter spores to better fit them for their bandit life.

28b Thread-like parts alternating with swollen parts; wandering through several host cells. Family CLADOCHYTRIACEAE

Figure 149

Fig.149. Cladochytrium replicatum Karl.

This species grows as a parasite on several species of algae as well as on some aquatic seed-bearing plants.

29a Fertilization by motile sperms; zoospores with but one flagellum. Aquatic saprophytes. Order MONOBLEPHARIDALES
Family MONOBLEPHARIDACEAE

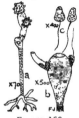

Figure 150

Fig.150. Monoblepharis polymorpha Cor.; a, plant with reproductive organs; b, antheridium, oogonium and uniflagalated sperm; c, zoospore.

These saprophytes are found in fresh-water pools.

29b Sperms non-motile; fertilization through an antheridial
    tube. Figs. 151 to 153. 30

ORDER SAPROLEGNIALES

30a Vegetative mycelia, thin hyphae of uniform diameter; zoo-
    sporangia usually globular and much broader than the mycelium;
    zoospores biflagellated. Often parasitic on plants.
                                              Family PYTHIACEAE

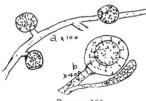

Fig.151. Pythium sp.; a, part of plant
with sporangia; b, antheridium and
oogonium.

It will be noted that the antheridia
(male organs) in these plants as well
as some others contact the eggs, making
it unnecessary for the sperms to be
motile.

Figure 151

30b Vegetative mycelia thick tubular hyphae; aquatic. Hypha
    not much thickened to form the cylindrical zoosporangia.
    Figs. 152 and 153. 31

31a Filaments with regular constrictions; often branched.
                                          Family LEPTOMITACEAE

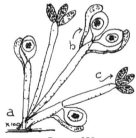

Fig.152. Sapromyces androgynus Thaxter;
a, part of plant with; b, antheridia
and oogonia and; c, sporangia.

The members of this family attach
themselves to the decaying plant parts on
which they live.

Figure 152

31b Filaments of uniform diameter not constricted. Often found
    growing on dead fish and other animals in water. Water Mold.
                                          Family SAPROLEGNIACEAE

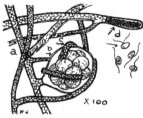

Fig.153. Saprolegnia sp.; a, coenocytic
filament; b, oogonium with eggs;
c, antheridium; d, sporangium and
zoospores.

These plants are known as "water
molds". They may be easily produced for
study by leaving dead insects in pond
water for a few days. The spores of
course are already in the water when it
is collected. That makes it desirable
to get water at several places.

Figure 153

32a Asexual reproduction by conidiospores. Some species parasitic on insects, others saprophytic. Figs. 154 and 155 . . 33

32b Asexual reproduction by means of aplanospores borne in sporangia. The Black Molds. Figs. 156 to 158 34

ORDER ENTOMOPHTHORALES

33a Parasitic on spiders and insects.   Family ENTOMOPHTHORACEAE

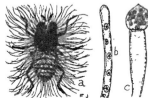

Figure 154

Fig.154. *Empusa muscae* Cohn.; a, Fly killed by this parasite; b, hypha from body of fly; c, conidiophore.

The flies found dead and attached to window panes, etc., have usually been killed by this fungus. A fly swatter is quicker and more certain, however.

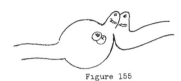

Figure 155

33b Parasitic on plants, or saprophytic.   Family BASIDIOBOLACEAE

Fig.155. *Basidiobolus ranarum*.

Mycelium with reproductive organs. This species grows on the dung of frogs.

ORDER MUCORALES

34a Asexual spores borne in typical sporangia. Figs. 157 and 158. 35

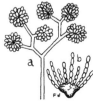

Figure 156

34b Asexual spores conidia-like, sometimes accompanied by larger sporangia with many spores. Conidiospores in chains.
Family PIPTOCEPHALIDACEAE

Fig.156. *Piptocephalis* sp.; a, conidiophore; b, conidial head with spores.

This fungus lives parasitically on other fungi.

35a Sporangium with a columella; zygospore but thinly covered or naked. A large family including the bread molds and many others.
Family MUCORACEAE

Figure 157

Fig.157. *Rhizopus nigricans* Ehr.; a, showing habits of growth; b, sporangium with columella; c, zygospore.

This is the mold that greets you when you open the bread box. Two strains are required if zygospores are to be produced.

35b Sporangium without a columella; zygospore surrounded by a thick wall of the hypha.   Family MORTIERELLACEAE

Figure 158

Fig.158. <u>Mortierella</u> <u>candelabrum</u>; a, branched sporangiophore; b, sporangium.

In this family both sporangiophores and conidia are often produced on the same plant.

THE SAC FUNGI (ASCOMYCETES)

36a Without definite fruiting bodies; asci formed directly from the zygote and borne singly on a mycelium. Sub-class PROTOASCOMYCETAE. Figs. 159 and 160 37

36b Asci contained in a definite fruiting body. Asci arising indirectly from the zygote. Figs. 161 to 185. Sub-class EUASCOMYCETAE. 38

ORDER SACCHAROMYCETALES

37a Asci similar to vegetative cells. Vegetative cells solitary or but loosely attached in strands scarcely forming a mycelium. The Yeasts.   Family SACCHAROMYCETACEAE

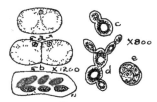

Figure 159

Fig.159. Fission Yeast, <u>Schizosac-charomyces</u> <u>octosporus</u> Bey.; a, vegetative cells; b, an ascus with ascospores; Budding yeast, <u>Saccharomyces</u> <u>cerevisiae</u> Han., c, budding cell; d, chain; e, ascus with ascospores.

Yeasts function not only in bread-making and the production of alcohol but also cause many food products to ferment and decay.

37b Asci terminal or intercalary on definite mycelia.
    Family ENDOMYCETACEAE

Figure 160

Fig.160. <u>Eremascus</u> <u>fertilis</u> Stop. Stages in reproduction.

Grows as a mold on jellies and other similar food products.

57

38a Asci grouped in a pallisade-like layer but not enclosed by a peridium.   **Order EXOASCALES**
                                                    Family EXOASCACEAE

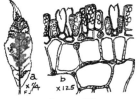

Fig.161. Exoascus deformans Fcl.; a, a diseased peach leaf; b, section through leaf showing asci.

Often common on peach trees but does not seem to do a great deal of harm.

Figure 161

———————— ⚭ ————————

38b Asci definitely related to a fruiting body (ascocarp) which may be widely open or nearly enclosed. Figs. 162 to 185 . . 39

39a Ascocarp (fruiting body) when mature, open and more or less cup-like (apothecium). Figs. 162 to 174 40

39b Ascocarp when mature, globular or cylindric enclosing the asci (perithecium). Figs. 175 to 185. 49

40a Apothecium disk, saucer or cup-shaped, with the asci standing parallel in a hymenial layer lining the cup; often closed when young; from very minute to 4 or 5 inches in diameter. Figs. 162 to 167 41

40b Fruiting tissue which is usually borne on a stalk exposed from the first, club-shaped or convex; with pits or ridges. Figs. 168 to 170 45

40c Fruiting tissue covered by a tough membrane and not becoming exposed until nearly mature. Figs. 171 to 174 47

40d Subterranean tuber-like fruiting bodies containing chambers in which the asci are borne. These truffles live on the roots of trees.   **Order TUBERALES**
                                                    Family TUBERACEAE

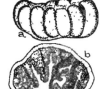

Fig.162. Tuber spp.; a, exterior view; b, cross section.

In Europe where these are much used for food, pigs and dogs are used to locate the truffles for digging.

Figure 162

ORDER PEZIZALES

41a Ascocarps leathery or horny, disk or plate-shaped and free from the first; paraphyses united to form a covering over the asci.   **Family PATELLARIACEAE**

Figure 163

Fig.163. <u>Patella</u> <u>scutellata</u> Morg.; a, as seen on bark; b, ascocarp in cross section; c, ascus.

On rotten wood or sometimes on soil, vermilion. Widely distributed.

41b Ascocarps waxy, fleshy or gelatinous, ends of paraphyses not uniting. Figs. 164 to 167 42

42a The outer coat of the asocarp (peridium) blending into the inner coat (hypothecium). Figs. 165 to 167. 43

42b The peridium and the hypothecium distinct; peridium of thin-walled translucent cells.   Family HELOTIACEAE

Figure 164

Fig.164. <u>Sclerotinia</u> <u>fructicola</u> Rehm.; American Brown Rot. A very destructive disease of stone fruits; a, apothecia growing on "mummy" plums; producing ascospores, b, conidiophores and conidia as they grow in great abundance on the decaying fruit.

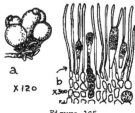

Figure 165

43a Fruiting layer of ascocarp, convex, and open from the first with little or no peridium.   Family PYRONEMACEAE

Fig.165. <u>Pyronema</u> <u>confluens</u> Obs.; a, oogonia and antheridia; b, cross section through young apothecium.

Common and widely distributed on charcoal in burned-over ground.

43b Fruiting layer of the ascocarp, concave with a fleshy peridium. Figs. 166 and 167 44

44a Upper surface of hymenial (fruiting) layer smooth without the asci standing above the rest of the layer. Apothecia either stalked or sessile.   Family PEZIZACEAE

Figure 166

Fig.166. <u>Peziza</u> <u>repanda</u> Pers.

Diameter up to 4 inches, whitish outside, pale brown within.

**44b Asci when mature projecting above the rest of the hymenial
layer. Apothecium without stalk.   Family ASCOBOLACEAE**

Figure 167

Fig.167. <u>Ascobolus</u> <u>magnificus</u> Dodge.

Diameter 1/5 to 1 inch; brownish when mature.

ORDER HELVELLALES

**45b Ascocarp without stalk, often attached by several rhizome-
like strands of mycelia; fleshy or waxy.   Family RHIZINACEAE**

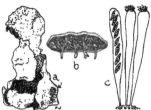

Figure 168

Fig.168. <u>Rhizina</u> <u>inflata</u> Karst.;
a, top view; b, lower view; c, asci.

Diameter up to one inch; brown.

**46a Fertile part of the fleshy fruiting body an enlarged head,
yellow, green or black; asci opening by a slit or pore. The
Earth Tongues.   Family GEOGLOSSACEAE**

Figure 169

Fig.169. a, <u>Mitrula</u> <u>vitellina</u> Pk. In
mossy places. Height to 2 inches, pale
yellow. b, <u>Geoglossum</u> <u>hirsutum</u>, 2 to 3
inches high, black, surface covered with
hairs.

**46b Fruiting body a fleshy roughened head growing on a hollow
stalk. Asci club-shaped and opening at the end by a cap.
                                      Family HELVELLACEAE**

Figure 170

Fig.170. a, <u>Morchella</u> <u>esculenta</u>
Pers, Common Morel, 1 to 4 inches
high, fruits in the spring, edi-
ble; b, <u>Gyromitra</u> <u>esculenta</u> Fr.,
Edible Gyromitra, stem whitish,
cap dark red, 2 to 5 inches high;
c, <u>Helvella</u> <u>lacunosa</u> Afz., Black-
capped Helvella, June to October,
1 to 3 inches high, black, edible.

47a Fruiting ascocarp elongate, opening by a fissure running
    lengthwise. Figs. 172 to 174. 48

47b Fruiting ascocarp rounded, opening by radiating or star-
    shaped fissures.   Order PHACIDIALES

      Ascocarps leathery, black and remaining sunken in the tissue
    of the host.   Family PHACIDIACEAE

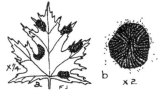

Fig.171. <u>Rhytisma acerinum</u> Fr., Leaf-
    blotch. A parasite causing black
    leaf-spots on maples.; a leaf with
    spots; b, ascocarp.

Figure 171

ORDER HYSTERIALES

48a Ascocarp covered by other tissue, its walls attached to its
    covering.   Family HYPODERMATACEAE

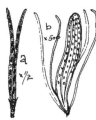

Fig.172. <u>Lophodermium pinastri</u> Chev., produces
    a blight on leaves of the Scotch pine;
    a, leaves of pine showing blight spots;
    b, ascus and paraphyses.

Figure 172

48b Ascocarps free from the first; walls black; usually linear
    though sometimes round, oval or shield-shaped.
                                              Family HYSTERIACEAE

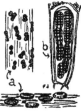

Fig.173. <u>Hysterographium froxini</u> DeN. Common
    and widely distributed on Ash.; a, Twig of
    host with fruiting bodies; b, ascocarps, en-
    larged; c, ascus with ascospores.

Figure 173

49a Microscopic fungi living on insects as parasites; perithecia
    stalked.   Order LABOULBENIALES
                                          Family LABOULBENIACEAE

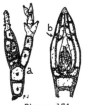

Figure 174

Fig.174. <u>Stigmatomyces</u> <u>baerii</u> Peyri.; a, mature plant; b, perithecium with asci.

Apparently not very common.

49b Perithecium not stalked, solitary and free or united and enclosed in a supporting body. Figs. 175 to 185 50

50a Asci arranged irregularly within the perithecium.
Order ASPERGILLALES

Ascocarps mostly sessile; and never submerged; mostly saprophytic and spreading asexually by conidiospores which are produced in extraordinary abundance. Many colors and shades.
Family ASPERGILLACEAE

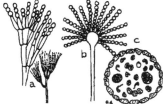

Figure 175

Fig.175. <u>Penicillium</u> <u>commune</u>;
a, conidial head showing spore
formation; <u>Aspergillus</u> sp.;
b, typical conidial head; c, section through ascocarp showing
asci.

50b Asci forming at a uniform level. Figs. 176 to 185. . . . 51

51a Perithecium globular, scattered and with no opening. Ex-
ternal parasites. Figs. 176 and 177 52

51b Perithecium with opening. Figs. 178 to 185 53

ORDER ERYSIPHALES

52a Mycelium white; appendages extending from perithecium.
Powdery Mildews.   Family ERYSIPHACEAE

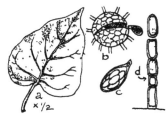

Figure 176

Fig.176. <u>Microsphaera</u> <u>alni</u>, Powdery
Mildew of Lilac; a, leaf of Lilac
showing the mildew; b, perithecium
showing asci; c, an ascus;
d, conidiophore.

Powdery mildews are exceedingly
common, particularly in damp seasons.

**52b Outer mycelia dark colored. Perithecia without true append-
ages.   Family PERISPORIACEAE**

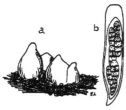

Fig.177. <u>Apiosporium</u> <u>salicinum</u> Kze.;
a, plant with perithecia; b, ascus.

Grows on the leaves of trees and
shrubs.

Figure 177

**53a Perithecium bright colored, fleshy or membranous.
                                       Order HYPOCREALES
                                       Family HYPOCREACEAE**

Fig.178. <u>Claviceps</u> <u>purpurea</u> Tul.; a, head of
rye with ergoted grains; b, diseased grain
(sclerotium) developing ascocarps; c, section through ascocarp, showing asci.

The drug ergot is used in medicine.

Figure 178

53b Perithecium dark colored and hard. Figs. 179 to 185. . . 54

**54a Perithecium dark colored and distinct from the rest of the
mycelium. Figs. 180 to 185. . . . . 55**

**54b Perithecia imbedded in the mycelium and not distinct from
it.   Order DOTHIDIALES
                                       Family DOTHIDIACEAE**

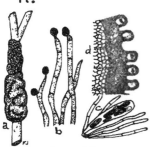

Fig.179. <u>Plowrightia</u> <u>morbosa</u> Sac., Black-
knot of Cherry; a, twig with diseased
growth; b, conidia; c, ascus; d, section bearing perithecia.

This disease attacks both our cultivated and wild cherries and many of our
plums.

Figure 179

ORDER SPHAERIALES

**55a Perithecia borne within a stroma (special supporting body).
Figs. 184 and 185. . . . . 59**

55b **Plants without a stroma.** **Figs. 180 to 183.** 56

56a **Perithecia free upon the substratum or enclosed at their base by a mycelial growth.** **Family SPHAERIACEAE**

Figure 180

Fig.180. <u>Rosellinia</u> <u>radiciperda</u> Mas.; a, fungus on host (cabbage); b, perithecium enlarged; c, conidiophore; <u>Trichosphaeria</u> <u>sacchari</u> Mas.; d, fungus on sugar cane; e, perithecia enlarged; f, conidiophores and spores.

56b **Perithecium usually wholly covered by the mycelium or epidermis of the host** 57

57a **Perithecium usually with a beak; its wall tough and leathery; asci thickened at apex and opening through a pore.** **Family GNOMONIACEAE**

Figure 181

Fig.181. <u>Glomerella</u> <u>rufomaculans</u> S.& V., Bitter-rot of Apple and other fruits; a, diseased apple; b, damage to a twig; c, perithecium with asci; d, conidial stage.

57b **Perithecium without a distinct beak; not darkened with carbon** 58

58a **Asci attached to walls of the perithecium; joined together in bunches but with no paraphyses.** **Family MYCOSPHAERELLACEAE**

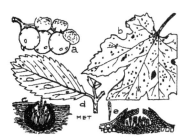

Figure 182

Fig.182. <u>Guignardia</u> <u>bidwellii</u> V.& R., Black-rot of Grapes; a, diseased fruit; b, diseased leaf; c, perithecium with asci (from diseased fruit); <u>Mycosphaerella</u> <u>fragariae</u> Lind., Leaf-spot of Strawberry, d, diseased leaf; e, perithecium on the host leaf.

58b Asci attached singly to the base of the perithecium; surrounded by paraphyses.   Family PLEOSPORACEAE

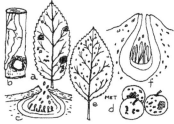

Figure 183

Fig.183. <u>Physalospora</u> <u>malorum</u> Shear., Black-rot of Apple and other Pome fruits; a, leaf with diseased spots; b, effect on twigs; c, section through perithecium; <u>Venturia</u> <u>pomi</u> Wint., Apple Scab; d, scab on apples; e, disease spots on a leaf; f, perithecium on leaf.

59a Host and parasite tissues intermingled in the stroma; conidiaspores borne in pycnidia.   Family VALSACEAE

Figure 184

Fig.184. <u>Valsa</u> sp.; a, fruiting bodies on limb of host; b, perithecium; c, asci.

59b Stroma of fungus tissue only. Spores blackish, almost always one-celled.   Family XYLARIACEAE

Figure 185

Fig.185. <u>Xylaria</u> sp.; a, Fruiting body (stroma); b, cross section through stroma showing perithecia; <u>Daldinia</u> sp.; c, stroma on a diseased branch; d, section through stroma showing perithecia in outer margin.

÷ | THE CLUB FUNGI (BASIDIOMYCETES) | ÷

60a Basidia four-celled, arising directly from resting spores and not forming a hymenium. (Closely associated in a definite structure). Parasitic. Other types of spores often formed, also. Figs. 186 to 189. (Sub-class HEMIBASIDII) 61

60b Basidia developing directly from vegetative cells and growing in groups in a hymenium. A few are parasites; mostly saprophytic. Figs. 190 to 200. (Sub-class EUBASIDII) 64

61a Great masses of usually black spores (chlamydospores) produced on the host plant, often on the floral parts, especially
the ovaries of the grasses. The chlamydospores germinate to
vegetative mycelia usually confined to interior of host tissue.
Figs. 186 and 187. (The Smuts) 62

61b Chlamydospores, if present borne on definite stalks; usually
absent. Basidia arising from teleutospores. Figs. 188 and
189. (The Rusts) 63

ORDER USTILAGINALES

62a Basidium (promycelium) with spores arising from the side at
or near the cross walls. These spores or sprout cells often
form budding chains.   Family USTILAGINACEAE

Figure 186

Fig.186. Corn Smut, Ustilago zeae
Ung.; a, infested ear of corn;
b, basidia with spores and sprout-
cells.

Very common in corn fields. May be
eaten like mushrooms when young.

62b Basidium (promycelium) with spores clustered at end.
                                          Family TILLETIACEAE

Figure 187

Fig.187. Stinking Smut, Tilletia tritici
Wint.; a, clamydospore having germin-
ated and the promycelium produced
spores which are conjugating and forming conidia; b, infected head of wheat.
Common on wheat.

ORDER UREDINALES

63a Teliospores without stalks; 1 to 4 celled.
                                          Family MELAMPSORACEAE

Figure 188

Fig.188. Cronartium ribicola Fischer,
White Pine Blister Rust; a, Gooseberry leaf and teliospores;
b, Gooseberry leaf and uredinio-
spores; c, stem of White Pine and
aeciospores.

Very destructive to our White
Pine forests.

63b Teliospores borne on a simple or compound stalk.
                                          Family PUCCINIACEAE

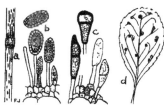

Figure 189

Fig.189. Puccinia graminis Pers., Black Stem Rust of Wheat; a, infected wheat stem; b, uredinospores; c, teliospores; d, barberry leaf with rust spots.

This fungus disease costs immense sums some years to wheat producers. Barberry eradication has helped to control it.

64a Hymenium enclosed within the fruiting body (sporocarp) until they are mature. Figs. 198 to 200 71

64b Hymenium exposed on some surface part of the fruiting body. Figs. 190 to 197 65

65a Saprophytes with thin expanded fruiting bodies, gelatinous when fresh or wet, and thorny or leathery when dry. Basidia forked or divided into four cells. Figs. 190 and 191. . . . 66

65b Fruiting body of many forms, often umbrella-like or shelf-like; basidia club-shaped or somewhat cylinderical. Figs. 192 to 197 67

ORDER TREMELLALES

66a Fruiting body shaped somewhat like a human ear. Grows on decaying wood. Basidia divided transversely into four cells. Ear Fungi.   Family AURICULARIACEAE

Figure 190

Fig.190. Jews Ear, Auricularia auricula-judae Schr.

Often abundant in the fall.

66b Fruiting body irregular, trembling when moist; tough and horny when dry. The Trembling Fungi.   Family TREMELLACEAE

Figure 191

Fig.191. Tremella sp.

The jelly-like rather irregular masses constituting the fruiting bodies of this plant are of several colors but always somewhat translucent.

ORDER HYMENOMYCETALES

67a Hymenium (fruiting layer which bears the basidia) smooth.
Figs. 192 and 193. 68

67b Hymenium covering projections, folds or pits. Figs. 194
to 197 69

68a Sporophore (fruiting body) leathery, often small and indefinite in shape.   Family THELEPHORACEAE

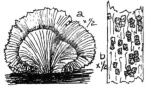

Figure 192

Fig.192. a, _Thelophora laciniata_ Pers.;
b, _Stereum frustulosum_ Fri.

Grows on the dead wood of oaks which
it disfigures.

68b Sporophore a single club-like part or much divided and
branched, usually fleshy; often resembling coral; delicately
tinted and colored. Coral Fungi.   Family CLAVARIACEAE

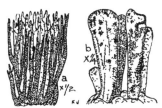

Figure 193

Fig.193. a, _Clavaria formosa_ Pers.;
b, _Clavaria pistillaris_ F., Indian
Club Clavaria.

Most of the members of this family
are edible.

69a Spore-bearing hymenium on suspended teeth or similar projections. Teeth Fungi.   Family HYDNACEAE

Figure 194

Fig.194. a, _Hydnum repandum_ Fr.; b, _Hydnum
coralloides_ Fr.

Both of these species are edible.

69b Spore-bearing hymenium covering the surface of gills (plate-
like structures hanging from under side).
                                             Family AGARICACEAE

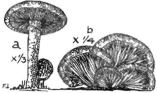

Figure 195

Fig.195. a, <u>Pholiota praecox</u> Pers.; b, Oyster Mushroom, <u>Pleurotus ostreatus</u> Fr.

Both of these species are edible. But if you are not sure of your identifications, you'd better be careful. Death is so permanent.

69c Hymenial layer forming the inner wall of pores. Figs. 196 and 197. . . . . **70**

Figure 196

70a Fruiting body fleshy; pores readily separating from their support. Family BOLETACEAE

Fig.196. <u>Boletus subaureus</u> Pk.

Yellow with blotches of red-brown; up to 4 inches in diameter. A valuable food species. Grows from early to late fall.

✓70b Fruiting body woody or leathery; pores not easily separating from supporting tissue. Family POLYPORACEAE

Figure 197

Fig.197. a, <u>Polyporus arcularis</u> Fr.; b, <u>Lenzites betulina</u> Fr., showing under surface.

ORDER GASTEROMYCETALES

71a Spore-bearing tissue enclosed in a membranous egg-like structure at first, but later breaking out and growing to some height. Spores adhesive. Plants with strong odor of carrion. Figs. 199 and 200. . . . . **72**

71b Spores remaining within the fruiting body until mature. Spores dry. The Puffballs, etc. Family LYCOPERDACEAE

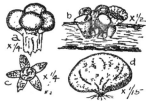

Figure 198

Fig.198. a, <u>Lycoperdon gemmatus</u> Bat.; b, <u>Cythus striatus</u>, Bird-nest fungus; c, <u>Geaster hygrometricus</u> Pers., Earth-Star; d, <u>Calvatia gigantea</u> Batsch.

As the species name indicates, this is a large one. Specimens 20 inches in diameter and weighing almost 20 lbs. have been found. All puffballs are edible.

72a Spores borne in a sticky mass (gleba) on the top of the stipe. The Stink Horn Fungi.   **Family PHALLACEAE**

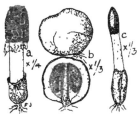

Figure 199

Fig.199. <u>Ithyphallus impudicans</u> Fr.; a, mature fruiting body; b, "eggs"; c, <u>Cynophallus caninus</u> Fr., Pink-capped Stinkhorn.

These have a way of making their whereabouts known. The flesh flies help spread the spores.

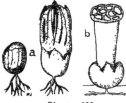

Figure 200

72b Spores borne within the receptacle which is split into a latticed design.   **Family CLATHRACEAE**

Fig.200. a, <u>Anthurus brownii</u>; b, <u>Simblum rubescens</u>.

The spores are borne within the fruiting body rather than on the outside as in the preceding family.

―――― ∽ ❧ ∾ ――――

THE BRYOPHYTA (LIVERWORTS AND MOSSES)

The keys for this entire section dealing with the Liverworts and Mosses have been made by Professor H.F. Conard of Grinnell College.

1a Plants growing flat, scale-like or ribbon-like, usually fork-branched, without distinction of stem and leaf; green or purplish. Figs. 202 to 204 and 206 to 212. Class HEPATICAE (in part) 2

1b Plants with stem and leaves; erect, ascending, prostrate, or hanging from trees. Figs. 201 and 213 to 224 3

2a Plant opaque by reason of air-spaces inside it; often showing air pores and polygonal markings. Rhizoids with pegs on the inside of the walls. Figs. 204 to 206. 5

2b Plant translucent, watery-looking, without inner air-spaces. Rhizoids without pegs. Figs. 202, 203 and 207 to 212. Class HEPATICAE (in part) 4

3a Leaves in two rows near upper side of stem, without midrib, and with cells isodiametric. Leaves very often notched at apex, or lobed, sometimes with a smaller lobe folded against a larger one. Sporophyte short-lived, the capsule raised on a stalk, splitting into four lobes, emitting spores and slender elaters with spiral bands. Order JUNGERMANNIALES ACROGYNAE. Figs. 201 and 213 to 224 10

Figure 201

3b   Leaves equally spaced all around the stem, usually with mid-
     rib; or in two opposite rows, with or without midrib; margins
     entire or toothed, never notched at apex or lobed; cells elon-
     gate to isodiametric. Sporophyte persisting for weeks or
     months. No elaters. Figs. 225 to 253. Class MUSCI. . Page 77

4a   Small rosettes of scales, with surface covered with pear-
     shaped sacs (involucres) each containing a capsule. No
     elaters.   Order SPHAEROCARPALES
                                           Family SPHAEROCARPACEAE

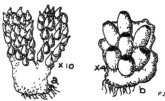

Figure 202

Fig.202. Sphaerocarpus texanus Aust.,
   a, male plant; b, female plant.

   The plants of this family and order are quite small and are found on
damp ground. The species name of the
example used here was given because
the type specimen came from Texas.
Species names usually have some such
significance.

4b   Larger (1 cm. or longer at maturity). Spores in a long rod-
     like capsule which splits in two above as it grows from the
     base, emitting spores and irregular elaters. No midrib and no
     gemmae, but sometimes the plant is rough. One chloroplast to
     each cell.   Order ANTHOCEROTALES
                                           Family ANTHOCEROTACEAE

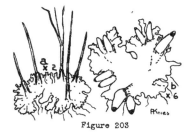

Figure 203

Fig.203. a, Anthoceros punctatus;
   b, Notothylus orbicularis.

   These plants are known as the
Horned Liverworts since the sporophyte has a horned shape. The
thallus is often an inch or more in
length.

4c   Spores in an oval or globular capsule on a slender watery
     stalk. Capsule splitting into four lobes, emitting spores and
     spiral-banded elaters. Midrib or mid-furrow distinct. Chloro-
     plasts numerous in each cell. Figs. 207 to 212. 6

ORDER MARCHANTIALES

5a   Air pores visible without a lens, each in a polygonal area.
     Capsules borne on the under side of an umbrella-shaped cap,
     with spirally banded elaters among the spores. Capsule wall
     cells with ring-shaped thickening.   Family MARCHANTIACEAE

71

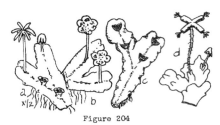

Figure 204

Fig.204. <u>Marchantia polymorpha</u> L. a, female plant; b, male plant; <u>Lunularia cruciata</u> (L); c, thallus with gemma cups; d, fruiting thallus.

The gemma cups with their asexual gemma-buds offer a unique scheme of multiplication. These tiny bits of the plant grow readily into a new thallus. The gemma cups of <u>Lunularia</u> are half-moon shaped.

5b   Air-pores not visible without a strong lens. Plants on moist or dry rocks and banks, rarely if ever in neat rosettes. Capsules as above, but with no ring-like thickenings.
Family REBOULIACEAE

Figure 205

Fig.205. <u>Reboulia hemisphaerica</u> G. L. & N.

This little liverwort seems to be scattered rather world-wide. It is found on rocks, walls and on the ground.

5c   Air-pores, if any, not visible with a hand lens. Plants submerged or floating, or in circular rosettes on very wet ground. Capsules imbedded in the plant, with no elaters among the rough spores.
Family RICCIACEAE

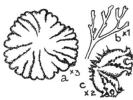

Figure 206

Fig.206. a, <u>Riccia frostii</u> Aust.; b, <u>Riccia fluitans</u> L.; c, <u>Ricciocarpus natans</u> (L.)

The members of this family are more simple than <u>Marchantia</u> but highly interesting.

ORDER METZGERIALES

6a   Plant deeply cut on both sides of a stem-like midrib into wrinkled leaf-like lobes.
Family FOSSOMBRONIACEAE

Figure 207

Fig.207. <u>Fossombronia pusilla</u> Dum.; a, plant; b, sporophyte; c, spores.

It grows along paths, ditches, etc., on moist ground. It is a small species.

6b   Plant with shallow marginal lobes, with lumps of blue-green algae embedded here and there, and with bottle-shaped gemma-containers, or tiny star-shaped gemmae.   On moist shaded banks. Family HAPLOLAENACEAE

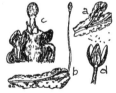

Fig.208. Blasia pusilla L., a, vegetative thallus; b, fruiting thallus; c, sporangium; d, capsule dehiscing.

Grows on damp clay or gravel; green to yellowish-green.

Figure 208

6c   Margins of plant even, or wavy but not regularly lobed. The plant itself may be variously lobed or branched. Figs. 209 to 212. 7

7a   Midrib well defined, bulging like a cord along lower side of plant, the rest of the plant only one cell thick. Figs. 209 and 210 8

7b   Midrib ill-defined; merely the gradually thickened central part of the plant, which is one cell thick only at the extreme margin if at all. Figs. 211 and 212. 9

8a   Plant 1 to 2 mm. wide, much longer than wide, of very even width. Sex organs underneath. On trees, leaves or damp ground. Family METZGERIACEAE

Fig.209. Metzgeria conjugata Lindb.

Widely scattered. Grows on tree trunks and rocks in shady places.

Figure 209

8b   Plant 3 to 4 mm. wide, often very irregularly lobed; sex organs on upper side, along midrib. On wet peaty ground. Family PALLAVICINIACEAE

Fig.210. Pallavicinia lyellii Gray, a, fruiting thallus; b, dehiscing capsule; c, antheridium.

Frequently submerged or on wet banks or in swamps. Widely distributed.

Figure 210

9a Plant 4 to 5 mm. wide, usually crowded in wide (10-50 cm.)
patches on moist ground. Elaters attached at base of capsule.
Family PELLIACEAE

Fig.211. _Pellia neesiana_ (Gott.).
a, fruiting thallus; b, male
thallus.

Green tinged with red along veins.
On wet ground. Widely distributed.

Figure 211

9b Plant 1 to 5 mm. wide, variously lobed or branched, in
shallow water or very wet places. Elaters attached to apex of
capsule (tips of valves).   Family ANEURACEAE

Fig.212. _Riccardia latifrons_ Lind., fruiting thallus.
Grows on wet decaying wood.

Figure 212

ORDER JUNGERMANNIALES

10a Leaves deeply divided into many threads or rows of cells.
Family PTILIDIACEAE

Fig.213. _Ptilidium ciliare_ Nees.;
a, fruiting plant; b, leaves enlarged;
c, involucre with dehiscing capsule.

Rather common; on stumps and rotten
logs.

Figure 213

10b Leaves entire, or toothed, or divided at tip into 2, 3, or
4 lobes. Figs. 214 to 224 11

11a Leaves flat or curved, not sharply folded. Figs. 214 to
219. 12

11b Leaves two-lobed and folded, one lobe pressed firmly against
the other. Figs. 220 to 224 15

12a Sporophyte borne in a perianth which is at the end of a distinct shoot. Figs. 214 to 217 13

12b Sporophyte borne from a small lateral or ventral bud; plants
easily seen, often large; perianth 3 angled with one angle ventral. Figs. 218 and 219 14

13a   Plants brown or purplish, in dense tufts on very wet rocks. Leaves with a rounded notch and two rounded lobes, set transversely on the stem. Perianth shorter than the surrounding leaves and grown fast to them.   Family MARSUPELLACEAE

Figure 214

Fig.214.   <u>Marsupella</u> <u>emarginata</u> Dum.; a, fruiting plant; b, tip of plant with involucral leaves; c, base of pedicel; dehiscing capsule.

On wet rock or floating in water. Usually restricted to mountain streams.

13b   Plants large (2 to 4 mm. wide) with leaves set very obliquely on the stem, succubous, with margins entire or sharply toothed.   Family PLAGIOCHILACEAE

Figure 215

Fig.215.   <u>Plagiochila</u> <u>interrupta</u> Dum.; a, fruiting plant; b, leaves in detail.

Occurs on moist banks and rotten logs.

13c   Leaves entire, or broadly and shallowly notched at apex. Underleaves deeply divided into two long slender sharp lobes (entire in <u>Harpanshis</u>). Perianth sharply triangular, with one edge upper.   Family HARPANTHACEAE

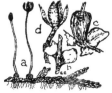

Figure 216

Fig.216.   <u>Chiloscyphus</u> <u>ascendens</u> H.& W.; a, plant with sporophytes; b, leaves in detail and antheridium; c, involucre; d, ripened capsule.

Found on decaying logs.

13d   Leaves entire or 2 or 3 lobed; underleaves entire or absent. Perianth oval or obovoid.   Family JUNGERMANNIACEAE

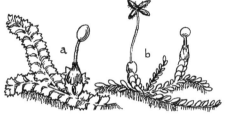

Figure 217

Fig.217.   a, <u>Jungermannia</u> <u>barbata</u> Sch.; b, <u>Nardia</u> <u>crenulata</u> Lin.

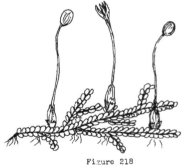

Figure 218

14a Leaves with two or more notches at apex (3 or more lobed); the upper margin of one leaf overlapping the lower margin of the above.
Family LEPIDOZIACEAE

Fig.218. Lepidozia reptans Dum.
Grows on soil and on rotten wood.

14b Leaves entire or two lobed. The upper margin of one leaf covered by the lower margin of the leaf above.
Family CEPHALOZIACEAE

Figure 219

Fig.219. Cephalozia multiflora Spr.
Grows on rotten wood and on the ground.

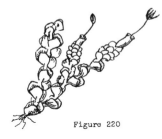

Figure 220

15a Upper lobe of leaf smaller than lower and only partly covering the lower.   Family SCAPANIACEAE

Fig.220. Scapania undulata Dum.
Leaves are reddish or purplish.

15b Upper lobe of leaf much larger than, and completely covering the lower. Figs. 221 to 224 16

16a Underlobe of leaf tongue-shaped, attached only at one end; under-leaf tongue-shaped, conspicuous. Large plants; 3 to 8 cm. long.   Family PORELLACEAE

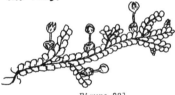

Figure 221

Fig.221. Porella platyphylla Lind.
On rocks and trees in moist places.

16b Underlobe forming a sac or pouch very narrowly attached
to upper lobe (or rarely tongue-shaped); underleaves present,
notched at apex. Several archegonia in each perithecium. Small
blackish or green plants 1 mm. wide or less.
                                            Family FRULLANIACEAE

Fig.222. Frullania asagraya Mont.

   Common; on rocks and bark of cone-
bearing trees.

Figure 222

16c Underlobe flat, its longest side attached to upper lobe.
Figs. 223 and 224 17

17a Underleaves absent; rhizoids attached in tufts to underlobes.
                                            Family RADULACEAE

Fig.223. Radula obconica Sul.

Figure 223

17b Underleaves present, entire or notched; rhizoids in tufts
attached to base of underleaf. One archegonium in each
perianth.   Family LEJEUNEACEAE

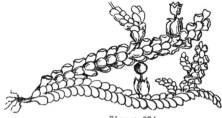

Fig.224. Lejeunea clypeata
Sul.; a, leafy plant;
b, leaves, top view;
c, leaves lower view;
d, sporophyte.

Grows on rocks and trees.

Figure 224

THE MOSSES (MUSCI)

1a Capsule raised on a pseudopodium, spherical, black, shedding
a round lid explosively. Leaves whitish, very porous and absorb-
ent. In bogs or wet places. (Peat Moss)   Order SPHAGNALES
                                               Family SPHAGNACEAE

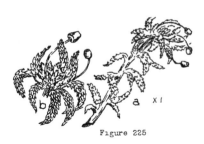

Figure 225

Fig.225. Sphagnum cymbifolium
Sedw.; a, plant; b, crown of
sphagnum plant bearing fruit.

This family contains but one
genus Sphagnum, of which there
are many species. The fruit is
rather scarce and is peculiar in
that its stem is a part of the
leafy plant instead of the capsule. This stem is known as a
pseudopodium. Peat used as fuel
is old, partly decayed sphagnum
taken from the bottom of bogs cut
into bricks and dried. The dry
plants are used for heat insulation and when moistened makes
ideal packing for growing plants.

**1b   Capsule raised on a pseudopodium, cylindric, brownish-black,
opening along the middle by four longitudinal slits. Leaves
minute, stiff, blackish, with very thick cell walls. On rocks,
in mountains. (The Black Mosses)   Order ANDREAEALES
                                        Family ANDREAEACEAE**

Figure 226

Fig.226. Andreaea petrophila
Ehrh.; a, leafy plant with
fruit.

All the members of this family are included in the one
genus, Andreaea. The plants are
very small, the slender fragile
stems standing usually not over
1/2 inch tall. The capsule
which has no lid divides into 4
vertical parts which diverge
when dry.

**1c   Capsule raised on a rigid seta or nestled among leaves of
the plant, dehiscent by a lid, or indehiscent. Of many colors
and textures, in all kinds of habitats. Figs. 227 to 253 . . 2**

ORDER BRYALES

**2a   Mouth of capsule beset with teeth in a single row, each of
which is made up of many cells; teeth without transverse bars
or lines. Figs. 228 and 229. . . . . .3**

**2b   Mouth of capsule with one or two rows of membranous teeth,
or without teeth, or capsules indehiscent. Teeth usually with
transverse bars or lines. Figs. 230 to 253 . . . . .4**

**2c   Peristome double, the inner being a conspicuous conical
plaited membrane, the outer of numerous rod-like rows of cells,
or rudiments of these. Capsules oblique and unsymmetric. On
banks rich in humus. Saprophytic.**
**   Family BUXBAUMIACEAE**

Figure 227

Fig.227. <u>Webera sessilis</u> Lin.

These plants are tiny, have but few or no leaves and in every way are strange-appearing mosses.

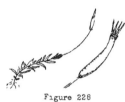

Figure 228

3a   Teeth 4, capsule cylindric. Leaves small, ovoid, pointed, with midrib and isodiametric cells. Some stems bear gemma cups at summit. On moist rotten wood, or on moist sandstone. Family TETRAPHIDACEAE

Fig.228. <u>Georgia pellucida</u> Rab.

No other mosses have such small number of peristome teeth.

3b   Teeth 32 to 64, their tips attached to a thin membrane covering the mouth of the capsule. Leaves with upright green lamellae along the midrib.
Family POLYTRICHACEAE

Fig.229. a, <u>Pogonatum brevicaule</u> Beauv.; <u>Polytrichum commune</u> L. Hair-cap Moss; b, plant with mature capsule; c, sporangium with calyptra.

The plants of this family are large for mosses and are among the most common mosses of most regions.

Figure 229

4a   Peristome consisting of a single row of teeth, each composed (at least at base) of two layers of plates; in the outer layer a single plate forms the width of the tooth; in the inner, two plates go to form the width of the tooth; hence, the tooth seen from <u>within</u> shows a fine longitudinal line. If without teeth or indehiscent, the leaf cells are elongate, pointed and smooth, or small, isodiametric and papillose, or small and very thick walled. Fig. 230. Sub-class HAPLOLEPIDEAE. . 5

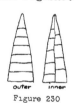

Figure 230

4b   Peristome characteristically in two circles; an inner thin membrane divided into <u>segments</u>, an outer of 16 (or 8) firm <u>teeth</u>. A tooth is composed (at least at base) of two layers of plates; in the outer layer two plates go to form the width of the tooth; the outer surface therefore shows a fine longitudinal line. In the inner layer a single plate forms the width of the tooth. If without teeth or indehiscent the leaf cells are large, isodiametric or sharply rectangular, and smooth walled. If inner peristome is lacking the structure of the teeth will tell. Fig. 231 . . .11

Figure 231

4c   Peristome single, double or none. Leaves tongue-shaped,
  papillose (hairy). Calyptra cylindric, long pointed above, completely covering the capsule.   Family ENCALYPTACEAE

Fig.232. <u>Encalypta</u> <u>strepto-</u>
    <u>carpa</u> (Hedw.)

The calyptra of these mosses
so resembles the extinguisher
of a candle that they are sometimes called "Extinguisher
Mosses".

Figure 232

5a   Peristome teeth 16, split at apex into two prongs; if peristome is absent the leaf cells are long, pointed and smooth, or
  small and thick walled. Figs. 233 to 253 6

5b   Peristome teeth 16, either undivided or, commonly, divided
  into slender threads which are more or less spirally twisted,
  or imperfect or absent. Upper leaf cells usually papillose,
  small, isodiametric. Calyptra not covering capsule, early
  falling off.   Family POTTIACEAE

Fig.233. a, <u>Tortula</u> <u>ruralis</u> Ehrb.;
    b, <u>Pottia</u> <u>truncatula</u> Lind.

The peristome teeth in <u>Tortula</u>
are usually twisted together.

Figure 233

6a   Teeth split half way down. Leaves in two opposite rows,
  each leaf being split at base and standing astride of the next
  younger leaf (equitant).   Family FISSIDENTACEAE

Fig.234. <u>Fissidens</u> <u>adiantoides</u>
  Hedw.

The leaves are arranged in one
plane. These plants reach a
height of about 1/2 inch.

Figure 234

6b   Leaves spirally arranged, over-lapping like scales of a
  cone. Figs. 235 to 253 7

Figure 235

7a   Harsh black or blackish-green mosses on
dry exposed rocks, sometimes in streams;
cell walls thick, often wavy. Leaves often
tipped with a colorless bristle. Peristome
teeth entire, cleft, perforate or lacking.
                    Family GRIMMIACEAE

Fig.235. a, Grimmia apocarpa Hedw.;
    b, Rhacomitrium aciculare Brid.

    These plants almost always grow on rocks.
The leaves often have transparent tips.

7b   Spores small and very numerous. Plants and capsules various. Figs. 236 to 253. 8

8a   Peristome teeth split nearly to the base into 2 slender
strands, or absent. Plants of soil or crevices of rock, medium
size to small. Figs. 236 and 237 9

8b   Peristome split half way. Leaves long, slender pointed,
erect or curved to one side. Medium sized to large mosses.
Figs. 238 to 253. 10

9a   Stem distinct, short or long; leaves with midrib. Peristome
present or absent.   Family DITRICHACEAE

Figure 236

Fig.236. a, Ditrichum pal-
    lidum Ham.; b, Pleuridium
    subulatum Rab., plant and
    sporophyte; Ceratodon pur-
    pureus Brid.; c, plant;
    d, peristome teeth.

    Some members of this fami-
ly attain a height of several
inches while others are very
small. Decaying wood, rocks
and soil are the usual
habitat.

9b   Stemless; a microscopic cluster of leaves enclosing an indehiscent capsule. Leaf cells rhomboid-hexagonal; midrib present
or absent.   Family EPHEMERACEAE

Figure 237

Fig.237. Ephemerum serratum Ham.;
    a, plant with protonema;
    b, sporophyte; c, Nanomitrium
    sp., single plant with sporo-
    phyte.

    The members of this family are
very small often less than 1/15
inch high. The protonema often
remains active.

81

10a Leaves firm without spongy empty cells.   Family DICRANACEAE

Figure 238

Fig.238. <u>Dicranum</u> <u>longifolium</u> Ehr.

Usually yellowish green with long slim leaves. Spores mature in the fall. Very common on rotting logs.

10b Leaves spongy, with 2 to 4 layers of large empty cells; the chlorophyll cells hidden in the angles. Capsules curved, ribbed, with a swelling on the concave side at base. Plants in dense whitish or pale green cushions.   Family LEUCOBRYACEAE

Figure 239

Fig.239. <u>Leucobryum</u> <u>glaucum</u> Schimp.

This species is known as the White Moss. Round, thick tufts of these gray-white plants are common in moist woods. The sporophytes are formed sparingly.

11a Inner peristome segments directly in front of outer (not alternating); if peristome is lacking, the leaf cells are rectangular with square ends, smooth. Hypophysis not noticeable.   Family FUNARIACEAE

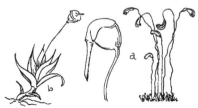

Figure 240

Fig.240. a, <u>Funaria</u> <u>hygrometrica</u> Sib. This has been called the Cord Moss. The stem of the sporophyte twists and untwists with changes of moisture; b, <u>Physcomitrium</u> <u>turbinatum</u> Brid. This "Common Urn-Moss" is up to 1/2 inch high.

11b Peristome single, but teeth with 2 rows of plates on outer surface. Hypophysis long or broad or both, often larger than urn, very conspicuous. Stems short, seta long. On dung or decaying vegetable matter at high altitudes or latitudes.
Family SPLACHNACEAE

Figure 241

Fig.241. <u>Tetraplodon</u> <u>bryoides</u> Lind.; a, typical plant; b, sporangium with calyptra; c, old sporangium; d, peristome teeth.

These mosses are confined in their growth to animal tissues or animal excrement. The greatly enlarged base of the sporangium (hypophysis) is a distinguishing character.

11c Peristome lacking. Capsules nearly erect and globular, small. Leaves in 2 rows, the shoot resembling a microscopic fern. Protonema perennial, in caves, glittering golden green by reflected light.   Family SCHISTOSTEGACEAE

Figure 242

Fig.242. <u>Schistostega osmundacea</u> Mohr., typical plant.

This species has been named the Luminous Moss. It grows in dark cavities and caves where it glows with reflected light. The species name refers to its fern-like leaves.

11d Inner peristome segments alternating with the outer. Order EU-BRYALES. Figs. 243 to 253 12

12a Sporophyte rising from the apex of a main shoot or main branch, with normal leaves around the base. Plants mostly erect. Figs. 243 to 248. 13

12b Sporophyte arising from a peculiar lateral bud whose leaves are very different from ordinary leaves. Plants mostly creeping and branching freely. Figs. 249 to 253 17

13a Inner peristome made of slender cilia alternating with 16 short broad outer teeth, the latter often united in 8 pairs.
Family ORTHOTRICHACEAE

Figure 243

Fig.243. <u>Amphidium lapponicum</u> Sch.; a, plant; b, sporangium with calyptra; c, sporophyte; d, an old capsule.

This is a family of tree-loving mosses. The plants are small and very dark green. The ridges on the dry capsules is a good family character.

13b Inner peristome a circle of prickly cilia. Stout erect mosses.   Family TIMMIACEAE

Figure 244

Fig.244. <u>Timmia</u> sp.; a, plant; b, mature sporangium; c, dry sporangium.

The family is small but the plants are fairly large. There is but the one American genus.

13c Inner peristome a cleft and perforated membrane. 14

14a Leaves papillose. Figs. 245 and 246 15

14b   Leaves smooth, not papillose. Figs. 247 and 248. 16

15a Capsules cylindric, curved, ribbed. Plants often topped by
     a naked stalk bearing gemmae. Leaves broad or narrow, not
     slenderly tapering.   Family AULACMNIACEAE

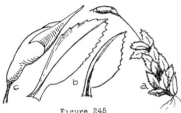

Figure 245

Fig.245. <u>Aulacomnium</u> <u>heterosti-</u>
     <u>chum</u> B.& S.; a, plant;
     b, leaf; c, sporangium and
     calyptra.

     The plants are green, and
brownish below. The habitat is
moist woods and bogs where it
grows on the ground.

15b Capsules globular, ribbed, erect but with lid obliquely
     placed. Leaves narrow to finely taper-pointed.
                                        .Family BARTRAMIACEAE

Figure 246

Fig.246. <u>Bartramia</u> <u>pomiformis</u>
     Hed.; a, plant; b, leaf;
     c, capsule and calyptra;
     d, dry capsule.

     Medium to large sized plants
belong to this family. They
grow in sizable tufts in damp
shady places.

16a Capsules pear-shaped, horizontal to nodding. Leaves broad
     to hairlike.   Family BRYACEAE

Figure 247

Fig.247. <u>Bryum</u> <u>capillare</u> L.;
     a, plant; b, leaf; c, capsule;
     d, dry capsule.

     Fairly large species usually
with broad leaves. A large and
important family.

16b Capsules barrel-shaped, symmetrical, nodding on a sharply
     bent seta. Leaves broad, with isodiametric cells. Stems often
     bending over and rooting at the tip.   Family MNIACEAE

Figure 248

Fig.248. <u>Mnium</u> <u>affine</u> Bland.;
     a, male plant; b, female plant;
     c, leaf; d, dry capsule, and
     peristome teeth.

     The plants of this family are
still larger than those of the
preceding one.

17a Inner peristome more or less incomplete or even absent;
     outer teeth with the diplolepideous structure. (See Fig.
     231). 18

17b Inner peristome well developed, though cilia may be absent
     and each segment may be reduced to a double row of plates.
     Figs. 252 and 253 20

18a Aquatic; attached to stones or sticks, rarely free. Leaf
     cells long-linear. Peristome with 16 outer teeth and an inner
     conical network. Seta short, barely equaling the capsule
     (Water Mosses).   Family FONTINALACEAE

Fig.249. Fontinalis lescurii Sul.;
a, portion of plant; b, sporophyte; c, mature capsule showing
peristome; d, leaf.

Purely aquatic, attached at base
with long stems floating.

Figure 249

18b On trees or rocks, never in water. 19

19a Leaves spirally arranged all round the stem; capsule without
     inner peristome.   Family LEUCODONTACEAE

Fig.250. Forsstraemia tri-
chomitria Lin., a, part of
plant; b, capsule with calyptra; c, capsule with operculum;
d, leaf.

The members of this family
are almost wholly confined to
trees.

Figure 250

19b Leaves in 2 opposite rows, the twigs therefore flat.   Seta
     short. Capsule erect and symmetric or nearly so.
                                            Family NECKERACEAE

Fig.251. Neckera sp.; a, fruiting
plant; b, leaf. Habitat; rocks
and trees.

Figure 251

20a Leaves with papillae over the cell-cavity. Cells usually
     minute and indistinct.   .   Family LESKEACEAE

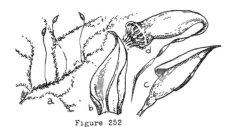

Figure 252

Fig.252. <u>Leskea polycarpa</u>
Ehrh.; a, plant; b, leaf;
c, fresh capsule with
calyptra; d, dry capsule.

A large family whose spe-
cies vary rather widely in
habitat, size, and form.

Figure 253

**20b   Leaves smooth, or papillose
by projecting ends of cell
walls. Cells usually distinct,
often very long and slender.
Family HYPNACEAE**

Fig.253. <u>Brachythecium oxycladon</u>
J.& S.; a, plant; b, leaf;
c, capsule; d, dry capsule.

Plants creeping on decaying
wood, etc., often fern-like.

THE PTERIDOPHYTA (FERNS)

**1a   Rush-like plants with the cylindrical stems jointed; their
nodes collared, with toothed sheaths. Spores borne in terminal
cone-like bodies.   Order EQUISETALES
                              Horsetail Family, EQUISETACEAE**

Figure 254

Fig.254. <u>Equisetum arvense</u> L. Field Horse-
tail. a, fertile shoot; appears in early
spring, pinkish brown, 5 to 10 inches high;
b, green vegetative shoot; appears after
fertile shoot, much branched, sometimes
reaching 2 ft. in height; c, <u>Equisetum ro-
bustum</u> A. Br., Stout Scouring-rush.

The stems of these interesting plants are
hollow. They are so heavily impregnated with
silica that they were once used for polishing.
One tropical species attains a height of 25 ft.
Less than fifty species are known.

1b   Stems, if any, neither collared nor conspicuously jointed. 2

ORDER FILICALES

**2a   Small floating plants with two-
ranked flat leaves. Large megaspores
and small microspores borne in separate bulb-like fruiting bodies clustered on underside of stem.
Salvinia Family SALVINIACEAE**

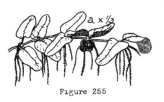

Figure 255

Fig.255. <u>Salvina natans</u> (L.), Floating Moss; a, plant showing roots and
leaves and fruiting bodies.

2b   Terrestrial or partly submerged plants but not floating. . 3

3a   Ferns with distinct tree-like trunks. In greenhouse or
      tropics.   Tree-Fern Family, CYATHEACEAE

Fig.256. Dicksonia antarctica Lab.

A native of Australia; attains a height of
30 feet with leaves 6 feet or more in length.

Tree-ferns are mostly natives of the tropics
or the southern hemisphere. They are palm-like
in general appearance but bear spores on the
underside or edges of the leaves. Some species
attain a height of 50 feet or more. Some 300
species are known.

Figure 256

3b   Not tree-like. 4

4a   Plants with creeping stems rooted in mud; leaves resembling
      4 leaf clovers. (The Pepperworts)
                                  Water-Fern Family, MARSILEACEAE

Fig.257. Marsilea quadrifolia L.,
European Pepperwort.

In shallow lakes or streams 2" to
10" high. The ovoid fruiting bodies
grow from the submerged stem and
produce both microspores and megaspores.

Figure 257

4b   Not habitually growing in water. 5

5a   Fruiting bodies borne on the back (Fig. 259a) or margins
      (Figs. 259b and c) of the vegetative leaves or on specialized
      fertile fronds (Fig. 257). Spores all alike. 6

5b   Spores borne in the axils of narrow, usually imbricated
      leaves. Stems thickly clothed with small moss-like leaves or
      leaves quill-like. (The Club Mosses and Quillworts). 9

6a   Twining vine-like ferns or small grass-like plants with
      spores borne in narrow pinnate spikes.
                              Climbing Fern Family, SCHIZAEACEAE

Fig.258. a, Lygodium palmatum
(Bernh.), Climbing Fern, found in
Eastern U. S.; b, Schizaea pusil-
la Pursh., Curly-grass.

Most of the members of this family are tropical, some of which are
found in greenhouses.

Figure 258

87

6b   Not as in 7a. 7

7a   Young leaves coiled, Fig. 259 8

Figure 259

7b   Young leaves not coiled; fruiting bodies in
a spike or panicle,the sporangia opening by a
transverse slit.   Adder's Tongue Family, OPHIOGLOSSACEAE

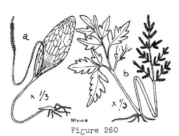

Figure 260

Fig.260. a, Ophioglossum vulgatum
L., Adder's Tongue; b, Botrychium
obliquum Muhl., Grape Fern.

These simpler ferns are rarer
than many others. They should be
protected wherever found.

8a   Sporangia opening vertically (Fig. 261c).
Flowering Fern Family, OSMUNDACEAE

Figure 261

Fig.261. a, Osmunda regalis L.,
Royal Fern; b, Osmunda claytoni-
ana L., Interrupted Fern.

Both of these ferns sometimes attain a height of 6 feet and are
widely distributed. The Interrupted
Fern is so called because of the
fertile pinnae. (Fig. 261d). These
become brown and withered presently.
We have had these sent in by persons
who thought this was a fungus disease and who were seeking a remedy.
Of course the prescription must be
"Raise some other species of fern".

8b   Sporangia opening transversely. The sporangia are stalked
and have a raised vertical ring (annulus). They are borne in
clusters (sori) on the back of the leaves (sometimes at the
leaf margin). Almost all of our common erect ferns belong
here.   Common Fern Family, POLYPODIACEAE

Figure 262

Fig.262. a, Asplenium filix-
foemina (L.), Lady Fern. Common throughout much of our
country; b, Adiantum pedatum
L., Maiden-hair Fern. A well-
known beautiful deep woods
fern; c, Pellaea atropurpurea
(L.), Purple-stemmed Cliff-
brake. Grows in crevices on
limestone bluffs.

Ferns are highly favored as
ornamentals yet some species become serious weed pests. There
are in all close to 5000 species
known in this family.

ORDER LYCOPODIALES

9a   Aquatic or mud plants; leaves hollow, cylindrical; stems short.

Quillwort Family, ISOETACEAE

Figure 263

Fig.263.   Isoetes engelmanii A. Br., Engelman's Quillwort.

The tapering quill-like leaves, 20 to 100, grow attached to a short fleshy stem and stand 8 to 15 inches high. It roots in mud with part of the plant usually submerged. Spores are of two kinds, as shown and are borne in a cavity in the leaf base.

9b   Terrestrial plants, leaves moss-like; stems elongate, creeping 11

10a   Spores all of one kind and size.

Club Moss Family, LYCOPODIACEAE

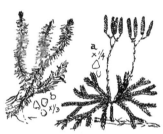

Figure 264

Fig.264.   a, Lycopodium complanatum L., Ground-pine. Erect stems arising 5-8 inches high from trailing stems several feet in length; b, Lycopodium lucidulum Michx., Shining Club-moss, 6 to 10 inches high.

A good number of the something over 100 species constituting this family are tropical, where many species live in trees (epiphytes); while others are terrestrial. Those in our region grow in deep damp woods. Club mosses are used for Christmas decorations and are often put into ornamental wreaths.

10b   Spores of two kinds and sizes, small microspores developing male gametophytes and quite large megaspores.

Little Club Moss Family, SELAGINELLACEAE

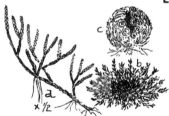

Figure 265

Fig.265.   a, Selaginella rupestris (L.), Rock Selaginella. Rather common on dry rocks, over 2 or 3 inches high; Selaginella lepidophylla, Resurrection plant; b, during rainy season; c, during dry weather. Rather common in the Southwest.

Some very beautiful members of this family are cultivated as "table ferns".

THE SPERMATOPHYTA (SEED-BEARING PLANTS)

1a   Ovules and seeds borne on the surface of a bract or scale; no stigma.   Figs. 266 to 269.   Class I GYMNOSPERMAE 2

1b   Ovules and seeds in a closed cavity (ovary) formed by the union of one or more modified leaves, the tips of which have developed into one or more stigmas for the reception of pollen. (Includes all of our common flowering plants). Class II ANGIOSPERMAE 4

→| THE GYMNOSPERMS |←

2a   Leaves pinnately compound; evergreen; trunk usually short and unbranched.   Cycas Family, CYCADACEAE

Figure 266

Fig.266. <u>Cycas revoluta</u> Thunb., Sago Palm; a, an old plant (female); b, a fruiting leaf with ovules.

This is not a true palm, of course, as the palms are Monocotyledons (see Fig.270). This cycad reaches a height of 6 to 10 ft. and its leaves a length of 2 to 7 ft. Cycads develop slowly. Fossil remains show that they were once very abundant. Younger plants have their leaves close to the ground.

Figure 267

2b   Leaves fan-shaped, deciduous on large spreading trees.   Ginkgo Family, GINKGOACEAE

Fig.267. <u>Ginkgo biloba</u> L., Maidenhair Tree; a, twig with dwarf branch, leaves and male flowers; b, fruit; c, female flowers and young fruit.

There is but this one species known for this family but it has found an important place as an ornamental tree.

2c   Leaves simple, scale-like, awl-shaped or needle-like; usually evergreen. Shrubs and trees. 3

3a   Seeds borne under the scales of dry cones or of somewhat fleshy berry-like cones.   Pine Family, PINACEAE

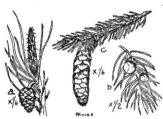

Figure 268

Fig.268. a, <u>Pinus sylvestris</u> L., Scotch Pine; b, <u>Juniperus communis</u> L., Common Juniper; c, <u>Picea canadensis</u>, White Spruce.

This is one of the highly important plant families as it contains many of our most valuable lumber trees.

Figure 269

3b   Seeds in a fleshy cup. Flowers single or in pairs. Trees or shrubs.   Yew Family, TAXACEAE

Fig.269. <u>Taxus bacata</u> L., English Yew. a, branch with fruit; b, fruit; c, young cone.

A tree reaching a height of 60 ft.; often cultivated. The Oregon Yew is a large forest tree while the American Yew (<u>Taxus canadensis</u>) is only a straggling shrub seldom attaining a height of 5 ft.

90

⇒ THE ANGIOSPERMS ⇐

4a   Leaves usually parallel-veined (a); flowering parts usually in 3's (b); stems hollow or with bundles scattered throughout (c); seeds usually with but one cotyledon. Fig. 270. THE MONOCOTYLEDONS.5

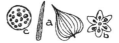

Figure 270

4b   Leaves usually net-veined (a); flowering parts usually in 5's (sometimes 4's) (b); stems with bundles arranged in a ring surrounding the pith, or woody with outer bark; seeds usually with two cotyledons. Fig. 271.   THE DICOTYLEDONS page 100

Figure 271

⇒ THE MONOCOTYLEDONS ⇐

5a   Plants with the palm-type of foliage, with large pinnate or palmate compound leaves.   Palm Family, PALMACEAE

Figure 272

Fig.272. a, Roystonea regia, Cuba Royal Palm, a native and much planted in Florida; b, Sabal minor, Dwarf Palmetto, in swamps, North Carolina to Texas; c, Washingtonia gracilis Par., a native of California.

This is a large family comprising almost 200 genera and more than 1500 species of mostly tropical evergreen plants. The majority are trees, some becoming quite large, but some members of the family are shrubs and others great climbers. The palms seen in greenhouses are usually juvenile plants and too immature to be easily determined to genus or species. The family yields many products of high economic importance. About 20 species of palms are native of the U.S.

5b   Plants not as in 5a. Figs. 273 to 302 6

6a   Small circular, oval or flask-shaped, plants floating free on water. No true leaves.   Duckweed Family, LEMNACEAE

Figure 273

Fig.273. a, Spirodela polyrhiza (L), Greater Duckweed; b, Lemna trisulca L., Ivy-leaved Duckweed.

These tiny plants produce flowers and seeds but one must look very close to see these structures. The winter is passed by sinking to the bottom of the pond.

6b   Plants not as in 6a. Figs. 274 to 302 7

7a   Flowers minute, surrounded by chaffy bracts (glumes); without a 3-parted perianth; flowers grouped in spikes or spikelets. Fig. 274. (The Grasses and Sedges) 8

Figure 274

7b   Flowers not in chaffy bracts or scales. Figs. 277 to 302. 9

8a   Leaves two-ranked (in two rows on the stem), the edges of their sheaths not united; stems cylindrical or flattened and almost always hollow; anthers attached by their middle; fruit a grain.   Grass Family, GRAMINEAE

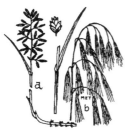

Figure 275

Fig.275.   a, Poa compressa L., English Blue-grass; b, Bromus tectorum L., Downy Brome-grass.

This is one of the largest and also one of the most important of all plant families. Removal of this family would cut off a very large percentage of the food crops of the world. Common examples: Corn, Wheat, Rice, Oats, Sugar Cane, Bamboo, etc.

8b   Leaves three-ranked (in 3 rows on the stem), the edges of their sheaths united; stems almost always triangular and solid; anthers attached at one end; fruit an achene.
                                                      Sedge Family, CYPERACEAE

Figure 276

Fig.276.   a, Carex aggregata Mack., Glomerate Sedge; b, Scirpus debilis Pursh., Club Rush; c, Cyperus erythrorhizos Muhl., Red-rooted Cyperus.

The sedges resemble the grasses in a superficial way. While they con- stitute a large family they are of comparatively small economic impor- tance though highly interesting.

9a   Flowers with only a rudimentary perianth, sometimes bristles or scales, or none. Figs. 277 to 280 10

9b   Flowers with sepals and petals (sometimes the two are quite similar). Figs. 281 to 302 13

10a   Flowers in a fleshy spike (spadix) (a^1) arising from an en- larged bract (spathe) (a^2).   Arum Family, ARACEAE

92

Figure 277

Fig.277. a, <u>Arisaema dracon-tium</u> (L), Green Dragon; b, <u>Acorus calamus</u> L., Sweet-Flag or Calamus.

The leaf-like part projecting beyond the flowering spike is the spathe. The drug calamus comes from the heavy root stalks of this plant. Common Examples: Calla Lilies, Elephant's Ear.

10b   Flowers not as in 10a. Figs. 278 to 280 11

11a   Submerged aquatic plants, leaves often floating.
Pondweed Family, NAJADACEAE

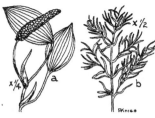

Figure 278

Fig.278. a, <u>Potamogeton heterophyllus</u> Schreb., Various-leaved Pondweed; b, <u>Najas flexilis</u> (Willd.), Slender Najas.

These are exceedingly important from the standpoint of maintaining a balanced condition of life in our water courses. They supply great quantities both of oxygen and of food for the many plant-feeding aquatic animals.

11b   Not normally submerged although usually growing in marshy places. Figs. 279 and 280. 12

12a   Flowers in elongate terminal spikes, fruit surrounded by bristles.
Cat-tail Family, TYPHACEAE

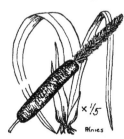

Figure 279

Fig.279. <u>Typha latifolia</u> L., Broad-leaved Cat-tail.

Cat-tails are found in marshes almost everywhere. Immense quantities of pollen is produced in the upper cylinder, while the lower part of one stalk may contain more than a million seeds.

12b   Flowers in spherical lateral spikes.
Bur-reed Family, SPARGANIACEAE

Figure 280

Fig.280. <u>Sparganium eurycarpum</u> Engelm., Broad-fruited Bur-reed.

This family contains but the one genus and only twenty some species. Most of the species are from one to 3 ft. in height but the species pictured may attain a height of 8 ft.

13a With perianth; carpels (one or more) distinct, at least when mature. Fig. 281 . . . .**14**

Figure 281

13b Carpels, one or more, united into one compound ovary. Fig. 282 . . . . **15**

Figure 282

14a Petals and sepals similar, anthers long and narrow; carpels attached to each other until ripe.

Arrow-grass Family, SCHEUCHZERIACEAE

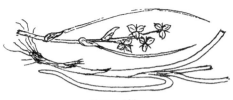

Figure 283

Fig.283. a, <u>Triglochin maritima</u> L., Spike-grass; b, <u>Scheuchzeria palustris</u> L.

This small family,- there are only some ten species known to science,- is of small consequence except that it must be accounted for somewhere.

14b Petals and sepals unlike, petals usually white; anthers short and thick; carpels separate.

Water-plantain Family, ALISMACEAE

Figure 284

Fig.284. <u>Alisma plantago-aquatica</u> L.; a, Water Plantain, grows in shallow water or mud.; b, <u>Sagittaria latifolia</u> Willd., Broad-leaved Arrow-head.

Many members of this family have leaves shaped like arrowheads, hence the name.

15a Ovary superior (hypogynous;-above the calyx). Fig. 285. . . . .**16**

Figure 285

15b Ovary wholly or partly inferior (epigynous;- below the calyx). Fig. 286 . . . .**21**

Figure 286

16a Some or all of the members of the perianth scaly, chaffy
bracts. Figs. 287 to 289 17

16b Not as in 16a. All members of the perianth leaf-like or
flower-like in texture. Figs. 290 to 302 19

17a Perianth of six chaffy, scale-like similar parts; leaves
grass-like; flowers small, perfect. The Rush Family, JUNCACEAE

Fig.287. a, Juncus tenuis Willd.,
Path Rush, Common throughout North
America. Watched by the Indians in
following old pathways; b, Juncus
brachycarpus Engelm., Short-fruited,
Rush.

Figure 287

17b Some of the perianth lobes chaffy, others not; herbs with
erect stems. Figs. 288 and 289 18

18a Flowers perfect (bisexual), yellow; in terminal scaly heads
or spikes.   Yellow-eyed Grass Family, XYRIDACEAE

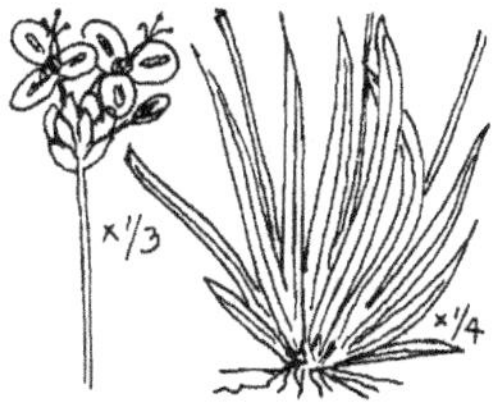

Fig.288. Xyris carolinana Walt., Carolina
Yellow-eyed Grass.

This species inhabits swamps and bogs
and is largely confined to the Atlantic
coast from Massachusetts south. Bogs form
the usual habitat of this small family
although an occasional species lives on
dry land.

Figure 288

18b Flowers imperfect (unisexual) in terminal scaly heads.
                              Pipewort Family, ERIOCAULACEAE

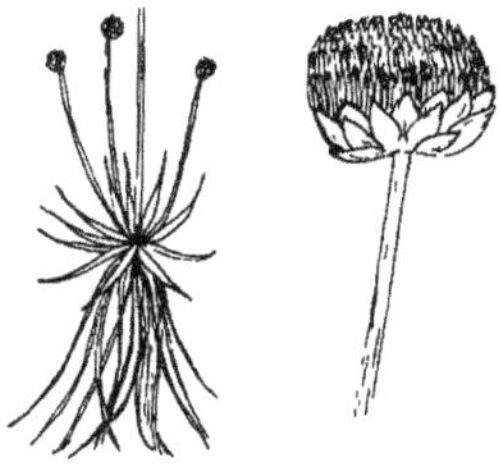

Fig.289. a, Eriocaulon articulatum
(Huds.), Seven-angled Pipewort.

The members of this family are usually
perennials and aquatic. They grow in
bogs or similar damp regions.

Figure 289

19a Terrestrial herbs. Figs. 292 to 302 20

19b Aquatic herbs, stamens 3 or 6 partly attached to perianth;
perianth of 6 parts all much alike, tubular.
                              Pickerel-weed Family, PONTEDERIACEAE

95

Figure 290

Fig.290. a, <u>Pontederia cordata</u> L., Pickeral-weed. Grows along streams and ponds; the flowers are bright blue; b, <u>Heteranthera dubia</u> (Jacq.), Water Star-grass.

Grows in water and occasionally along shore. Flowers are light yellow.

19c Plants usually epiphytic, often moss-like. Leaves and stems usually scurfy or mealy.

Pineapple Family, BROMELIACEAE

Figure 291

Fig.291. a, <u>Tillandsia</u> sp., Air Pine; b, <u>Dendropogon usneoides</u> (L.) Spanish Moss; c, <u>Ananas comosus</u> Merr., Pineapple.

Most of the members of this large family are confined to the tropics. The pineapple is one of the few members not ephiphytic. Florida (or Spanish) "moss" (it is not a moss of course) drapes a majority of the trees throughout the south. It is used for mattress and automobile upholstery.

20a Stamens usually 6; perianth of similar, mostly colored divisions (often more or less completely united); or 3 green sepals and 3 colored, withering persistent petals; plants often growing from bulbs; seed with horny endosperm.

Lily Family, LILIACEAE

Figure 292

Fig.292. a, <u>Lilium canadense</u> L., Nodding Lily; b, <u>Trillium grandiflorum</u> Sals., Large-flowered Wake Robin; c, <u>Asparagus officinalis</u> L., Asparagus.

Common examples: Onion, Garlic, and many ornamental plants.

20b Perianth of 3 persistent, usually green sepals and 3 ephemeral colored petals. Stamens 6, free; similar or dissimilar.

Spiderwort Family, COMMELINACEAE

Figure 293

Fig.293. a, <u>Commelina communis</u> L., Asiatic Day-flower. Flowers bright blue. Widely distributed. Introduced from Asia; b, <u>Tradescantia reflexa</u>, Ruf. Spiderwort.

The Spiderworts, very common both wild and in cultivation are showy plants. The Wandering Jew, a frequent ornamental belongs here.

21a Flowers dioecious (having only stamens or carpels [imperfect] but both kinds on the same plant). Figs. 294 and 295 22

21b Flowers perfect (both stamens and carpels in the same flower); ovules and seeds usually numerous. 23

22a Aquatic herbs. Stamens 3-12 sometimes united together; ovules and seeds several or numerous.
                              Frog's Bit Family, HYDROCHARITACEAE

Figure 294

Fig.294. a, <u>Elodea canadensis</u> Michx., Water-weed; b, <u>Vallisneria spiralis</u> L., Eel Grass. The above two plants are much used in aquaria as aerators and are sold for this purpose; c, <u>Limnobium spongia</u> (Bosc.), Frog's Bit. Flowers white.

22b Terrestrial twining plants; ovules and seeds but one or two in each of 3 cavities of ovary.   Yam Family, DIOSCOREACEAE

Figure 295

Fig.295. <u>Dioscorea villosa</u> L., Wild Yam-root.

There is but this one native species known for this family in the northern U. S. Some 200 species are found in warmer areas. Many of them grow large edible roots or above-ground tubers which make an important food contribution. (Some sweet potatoes are known as "Yams" but they belong to the family Convolvulaceae, Fig. 455).

23a Fertile stamens 3 or less. Figs. 298 to 302 24

23b Fertile stamens (maturing pollen) 6.
                              Amaryllis Family, AMARYLLIDACEAE

Figure 296

Fig.296. a, <u>Narcissus</u> <u>pseudo-narcissus</u> L. Daffodil; b, <u>Galanthus</u> <u>elwesii</u> Hook f., Giant Snowdrop; c, <u>Hippeastrum</u> <u>vittatum</u> (Herb.), Common Amaryllis.

At first glance the members of this family seem to be lilies but they differ in having the ovary below the flower instead of up in the flower as in the lilies.

23c Fertile stamens 5, sterile stamen (staminode) 1, not petal-like; plants with very large leaves.   Banana Family, MUSACEAE

Figure 297

Fig.297. <u>Musa</u> <u>paradisiaca</u> <u>sapientum</u> L., Banana.

The banana stalk attains a height of 15 to 30 ft. and bears one bunch of fruit when about a year old and then dies but the suckers grow into new fruit-bearing plants. Bananas may make the amazing yield of 100 tons per acre.

Other common example: Manila Hemp.

24a   Fertile stamens only one or two.   Figs. 298 and 299. . . .25

24b   Fertile stamens 3.   Figs. 300 to 302 26

25a   Stamens opposite the outer perianth segments; anthers facing outward and opening lengthwise.   Iris Family, IRIDACEAE

Figure 298

Fig.298. a, <u>Iris</u> <u>versicolor</u> L., Larger Blue Flag; b, <u>Sisyrinchium</u> <u>angustifolium</u> Mill., Blue-eyed Grass.

Over 170 species of Iris are known and innumerable varieties.

25b   Stamens opposite the inner perianth segments; anthers usually versatile.   Perianth woolly.
Bloodwort Family, HAEMODORACEAE

Fig.299. <u>Lachanthes</u> <u>tinctoria</u> (Walt.), Red-root.

In swamps along eastern part of our country; flowers yellow.

Figure 299

26a Stamens separate from the carpels. Figs. 301 and
 302 27

26b Stamens 1 or 2 united with the carpels. Flowers bilaterally symmetrical or very irregular; seeds fine and numerous.
                                      Orchid Family, ORCHIDACEAE

Fig.300. a, <u>Cypripedium</u> <u>hirsutum</u> Mill., Large Yellow Lady's Slip-per; b, <u>Liparis</u> <u>loeselii</u> Rich., Fen Orchis.

This family likely has more species than any other family of plants. More than 15,000 species are now known. The majority are tropical and many are epiphytic.

Figure 300

27a Ovules many in each cell; fruit a capsule with hard spherical seeds. Fertile stamens one with one or more sterile petal-
 like stamens.   Canna Family, CANNACEAE

Fig.301. a, <u>Canna</u> <u>indica</u> L., Indian Shot, flowers small, leaves very large; b, <u>Canna</u> generalis Bailey, Common Flowering Canna.

Figure 301

27b Ovules but one in each cell; fruit a capsule or berry-like,
 1 to 3 celled. Fertile stamens 1, petal-like sterile stamens
 often 5.   Arrowroot Family, MARANTACEAE

99

Figure 302

Fig.302. Maranta leuconeura Morr.

An ornamental from Brazil, prized for its showy leaves.

Common example: Arrowroot (Maranta arundinacea L.) a source of tapioca.

⇒ THE DICOTYLEDONS ⇐

1a Corolla (petals) none; calyx (sepals) present or absent, sometimes colored and resembling a corolla. Figs. 303 to 331 2

1b Both calyx and corolla present, at least in the staminate or perfect flowers. Figs. 332 to 472. 25

2a Trees with branches jointed resembling equisetum; only minute scales for leaves.   Casuarina Family, CASUARINACEAE

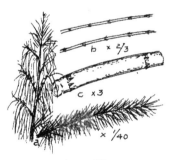

Figure 303

Fig.303. Casuaria equisetifolia L., Beefwood, Australian Pine. a, branches with long hair-like green stems; b, and c, sections of young stems showing scale-like leaves.

These trees are native of the Australian region but are extensively planted in our southern states for ornament, windbreaks, etc. Rapid growers; wood hard.

2b Plants with normal stems and leaves. Figs. 304 to 331 . . 3

3a Calyx present; sepals distinct or united, green or colored. Figs. 312 to 331. 9

3b Without a perianth (though a cup, gland or minute border may be present in the place of a calyx). Figs. 304 to 311. . . . 4

4a Herbs fairly large and sturdy (in marshes). Lizard's Tail Family, SAURURACEAE

Figure 304

Fig.304. <u>Saururus</u> <u>cernus</u> L., Lizard's Tail.

This family has broad alternate leaves and 3-4 carpels in an ovary with 1 to 2 seeds in each carpel. The Pepper Family (Piperaceae) closely related tropical and greenhouse plants are distinguished by having but one seed in each ovary. It includes woody as well . as herbaceous plants.

4b   Small frail herbs growing in mud or water. Leaves entire, even though submerged.   Water Starwort Family, CALLITRICHACEAE

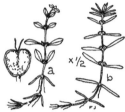

Figure 305

Fig.305. <u>Callitriche</u> <u>palustris</u> L., Water Fennel; a, terrestrial form; b, when submerged.

This family has but one genus. Some grow on wet soil, others in water.

4c   Submerged aquatic plants with finely divided leaves and minute flowers. Figs. 306 and 307. 5

4d   Trees or shrubs; staminate and sometimes the carpellate flowers in aments (slender spike of flowers). Figs. 308 to 311 6

5a   Plants 1 to several feet in length with finely cut whorled leaves; stamens many, sessile. An involucre (a) cut into many parts may be mistaken for a calyx.
                                    Hornwort Family, CERATOPHYLLACEAE

Figure 306

Fig.306. <u>Ceratophyllum</u> <u>demersum</u> L., Hornwort.

It is much used in aquaria for aeration. It is widely scattered in lakes and slow moving streams.

5b   Plants small, resembling moss or liverworts; stamens (but 2 in our genus) with filaments.
                                    River Weed Family, PODOSTEMACEAE

Figure 307

Fig.307. <u>Podostemum</u> <u>ceratophyllum</u> Michx.,
River Weed.

The flower arises from a cup-like spathe
with uncut edge. This olive green plant
grows in streams where it is attached to
the rocks.

**6a   Large trees with broad palmate leaves, the base of the
petiole surrounding the bud.   Plane-tree Family, PLATANACEAE**

Figure 308

Fig.308.   <u>Platanus</u> <u>occidentalis</u> L., Sycamore.

This family has but the one genus.   The bark
peels in large pieces from the upper limbs
leaving the branches a pale greenish-white.
Seeds are borne in round hanging spheres.   "a"
is the leaf of the London Plane sometimes
planted as an ornamental.

**6b   Trees and shrubs, but with axillary bud not covered by leaf
base. Figs. 309 to 311 . . . . 7**

**7a   Fruit many-seeded. Seeds when ripe carried by wind by tufts
of hairs at one end.   Willow Family, SALICACEAE**

Figure 309

Fig.309.   a, <u>Populus</u> <u>tremuloides</u> Michx.,
Quaking Aspen; b, <u>Salix</u> <u>interior</u>
Rowl., Sandbar Willow.

This is an important family of quick-
growing soft wood trees.   Much used for
firewood, cheap lumber, and training
small children.

**7b   Seeds not tufted for wind dispersal. Figs. 310 and
311 . . . . 8**

**8a   Fruit one-seeded; seeds without tufts of hairs, leaves resin-
dotted. Carpellate flowers solitary with but one carpel and
one ovule.   Bayberry Family, MYRICACEAE**

Figure 310

Fig.310. a, <u>Myrica gale</u> L., Sweet Gale.

A widely distributed shrub growing in swamps and along watercourses.

8b Carpellate flowers with compound ovary of two carpels. (Several united in a pendulous ball in the Sweetgum). Fruit a woody capsule. Witch Hazel Family, HAMAMELIDACEAE

Figure 311

Fig.311. a, Liquidambar <u>styra-ciflua</u> L., Sweetgum; b, <u>Hama-melis virginiana</u> L., Witch Hazel.

It will be noted that the flowers of this plant have both sepals and petals. They appear in late fall; the seeds mature a year later.

9a Flowers, at least the staminate, in aments. Figs. 312 to 315 10

9b Staminate flowers not in aments, but in clusters of different types, or rarely solitary. Figs. 316 to 331 14

10a Plants parasitic on trees; fruit a berry.
Mistletoe Family, LORANTHACEAE

Figure 312

Fig.312. a, <u>Phoradendron flavescens</u> (Pursh), American Mistletoe. Grows on several broad-leaved trees of East and South; b, <u>Razoumofskya americana</u> (Nutt.), American Dwarf Mistletoe. Parasitic on western pines.

The traditions relating to Mistletoe make it very helpful for the socially shy.

10b Plants not parasitic. Figs. 313 to 315 11

11a Both staminate and pistillate flowers in aments; neither a cup nor bur with the fruit. Birch Family, BETULACEAE

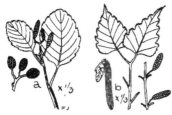

Fig.313. a, <u>Alnus tenuifolia</u> Nutt., Thin-leaved Alder. Along water-courses in West; b, <u>Betula populifolia</u> Marsh., American White Birch.

It is worth driving long distances just to see the great birch forests of our northern states and Canada.

Figure 313

11b Only the staminate flowers in aments. Figs. 314 and 315 .12

12a Leaves pinnately compound; fruit a nut with husk.
Walnut Family, JUGLANDACEAE

Fig.314. a, <u>Juglans nigra</u> L., Black Walnut; b, <u>Carya ovata</u> Koch., Shagbark Hickory.

This is a highly important family as it produces some of our most valuable woods and its nuts have good market value.

Figure 314

12b Leaves simple. Figs. 315 and 317. 13

13a Fruit a nut with bur or cup.   Beech Family, FAGACEAE

Fig.315. a, <u>Quercus alba</u> L., White Oak; b, <u>Fagus grandifolia</u> Ehrh., Beech.

The oaks produce some of our strongest timbers, finest finishing lumber and most beautiful trees. It is a grand genus.

Figure 315

13b Fruit a collection of tiny drupes uniting at maturity into a single somewhat-fleshy fruit (Mulberries, etc.). (See Fig. 317a).   The Nettle Family (in part), URTICACEAE

14a Ovary superior, flowers largely monoecious. Figs. 317 and 318 15

14b Ovary superior, flowers perfect. Fig. 316a 17

14c Ovary inferior. Fig. 316b . . . 16

Figure 316

104

15a Ovary 1-celled; fruit one-seeded. The Nettle Family, URTICACEAE

Figure 317

Fig.317. a, <u>Morus</u> <u>rubra</u> L., Red Mulberry; b, <u>Pilea</u> <u>pumila</u> (L.), Clearweed; c, <u>Ulmus</u> <u>fulva</u> Michx., Slippery Elm.

The American Elm is perhaps our most popular shade tree. Elms also furnish valuable lumber though not so desirable as oak.

15b Ovary usually 3-celled with one to 2 ovules in each cell; staminate and pistilate flowers on the same spike.
Box Family, BUXACEAE

Figure 318

Fig.318. <u>Pachysandra</u> <u>terminalis</u> S. & Z., Alleghany Mountain Spurge.

Common throughout our eastern mountains. The Common Box, an old world shrub or small tree, is a much prized ornamental which belongs to this family.

16a Ovary one-celled.
Sandalwood Family, SANTALACEAE

Figure 319

Fig.319. a, <u>Comandra</u> <u>pallida</u> A. Dc., Pale Comandra. Erect herb about one foot high partially parasitic on roots of other plants, flowers purplish; b, <u>Pyrularia</u> <u>pubera</u> Michx., Oil-nut, a shrub 3 to 15 ft. tall.

Sandalwood trees and shrubs, native of India and Australia, are sources of oil used in perfume.

16b Ovary several-celled (usually 6); flowers perfect.
Birthwort Family, ARISTOLOCHIACEAE

Figure 320

Fig.320. a, <u>Aristolochia</u> <u>tomentosa</u> Sims., Woolly Pipe-vine. The plant world has about 200 species of this genus. They are climbers for the most part and mostly woody. The flowers take peculiar shapes and in some species are large and highly colored. b, <u>Asarum</u> <u>canadense</u> L., Wild Ginger. A beautiful plant with velvety leaves and purplish-brown flowers. The stout rhizome has a strong odor of ginger.

105

17a Fruit an achene (dry one-seeded fruit); leaves simple; stems surrounded above each node by a stipular sheath.
Buckwheat Family, POLYGONACEAE

Fig.321. a, <u>Polygonum</u> <u>scandens</u> L., Climbing False Buckwheat; b, <u>Rumex</u> <u>altissimus</u> Wood, Tall Dock.

Common examples: Spinach-Dock, Rhubarb, Buckwheat, Prince's Feather, and many bad weeds.

Figure 321

17b Plants not as in 40a; embryo coiled, curved or ringed. Figs. 322 to 331. .18

18a Leaves alternate, simple, fruit a fleshy berry or drupe. Figs. 322 to 325. .19

18b Fruit not a fleshy berry. Figs. 326 to 331. 21

19a Ovary several celled. Fruit (in our species) a several-seeded berry with staining juice. Large herb. Ovary usually several-celled.　　　　Pokeweed Family, PHYTOLACCACEAE

Fig.322. <u>Phytolacca</u> <u>decandra</u> L., Common Poke.

The Indians used Poke berries for paint. They make a beautiful shade of magenta. The roots are said to be poisonous.

Figure 322

19b Ovary one-celled, one-seeded fruit a berry-like drupe; shrubs or trees. Figs. 323 to 325. 20

20a Leaves with translucent dots. Sepals 4-6; stamens 9 to 12. Aromatic trees or shrubs.　　　　Laurel Family, LAURACEAE

Fig.323. a, <u>Sassafras</u> <u>albidum</u> Nees, Sassafras;

The outer covering of the roots of the Sassafras tree furnishes the bark from which spring remedies have long been made. Sometimes called the "Mitten-tree" because of the shape of some of its leaves.

Figure 324

**20b Leaves with silvery, scurfy scales. Shrubs or small trees.
Sepals 4; stamens 4 to 8 (petals, in some exotic species).**
                                                 Oleaster Family, ELEAGNACEAE

Figure 324

Fig.324. <u>Elaeagnus</u> <u>argentea</u> Pursh., Silver-
     berry.

     Leaves, fruit and outside of flowers
silvery. Flowers yellow within. The
Russian Olive, a related species, makes a
valuable windbreak in northern regions.

Figure 325

**20c Shrubs with very tough bark. Calyx
     with 4 or 5 lobes or none. (Petals, in
     some exotic species).**
                           Mezereum Family, THYMELACEAE

Fig.325. <u>Dirca</u> <u>palustris</u> L., Leather-wood.

     The tough yellowish-green stems were used
by the Indians as cords for tying.

**21a Fruit a capsule, more than one-celled. (If only one-celled,
see Portulacaceae, Figs. 349 and 362, and Caryophyllaceae,
Figs. 373 and 396, which have a few species without petals).**
                                         Carpet-weed Family, AIZOACEAE

Figure 326

Fig.326. <u>Mollugo</u> <u>verticillata</u> L.,
     Carpet-weed.

     It grows very flat to the ground and
seems to do best where there is not
much competition. New Zealand Spinach
belongs to this family.

**21b Fruit a 1-celled capsule, a nut, or a drupe; with calyx, a
long cylindrical tube, usually swollen at base. Native in the
southern hemisphere and tropics.   Family PROTEACEAE**

Figure 327

Fig.327. <u>Hakea</u> sp.

     A fairly large family. Several
species such as the Silver Tree, Silk
Oak, Banksia and Queensland Nut are
planted as ornamentals.

107

21c Fruit not a more than 1-celled capsule. Figs. 328 to 331 .22

22a Calyx colored like a corolla; flowers in clusters surrounded
   by an involucre of distinct or united bracts.
                          Four-o'clock Family, NYCTAGINACEAE

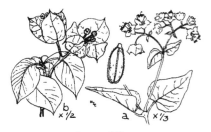

Fig.328. a, <u>Oxybaphus nycta-gineus</u> Sweet, Wild Four-o'clock, a rather common roadside weed with pink flowers; b, <u>Buginvillaea glabra</u> Choisy.

Some important ornamentals belong in this family.

Figure 328

22b Calyx not corolla-like. Figs. 329 to 331. 23

23a Leaves with scarious stipules (in one genus stipules absent,
   but stamens arise from margin of a hypanthium).
                          Knotwort Family, ILLECEBRACEAE

Fig.329. a, <u>Anychia canadensis</u> (L), Forked Chickweed; b, <u>Paronychia dichotoma</u> (L.), Forking Whitlow-wort.

These plants have tiny white or greenish flowers.

Figure 329

23b Leaves without stipules. Figs. 330 and 331. 24

24a Bracts dry, harsh and not green, perianth parts harsh, sharp-
   pointed.   Amaranth Family, AMARANTHACEAE

Fig.330. a, <u>Amaranthus retro-flexus</u> L., Red Root; b, <u>Gomphrena globosa</u> L., Globe Amaranth, a popular cultivated ornamental; flowers red, lavender, or white. They are dried and used in permanent bouquets.

Figure 330

24b Flowering parts and bracts usually soft and green; plants in
   many cases white-mealy.   Goosefoot Family, CHENOPODIACEAE

Figure 331

Fig.331. a, <u>Salsola pestifer</u> Nelson, Russian Thistle, a widely distributed serious pest from Europe and Asia. b, <u>Chenopodium album</u> L., Lamb's Quarters.

Common examples: Sugar and Garden Beet (same species), Common Spinach, and Summer Cypress.

25a Petals separated from each other. Fig. 332 .26

Figure 332

25b Petals at least partly united. Fig. 333. . 105

26a Ovary superior (sepals arising below the ovary). Fig. 316a 27

Figure 333

26b Ovary inferior or at least partly so, (sepals arising from sides or top of ovary). Fig. 316b 92

27a Carpels distinct, one to many. Fig. 334a 28

27b Carpels more than 1, united into a compound ovary. Fig. 334b. 39

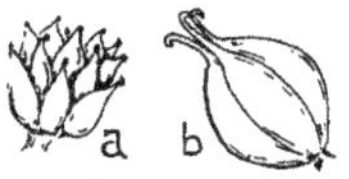

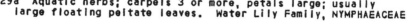

Figure 334

28a Stamens usually more numerous than the sepals and arising at the base of the ovary or below it; the sepals usually distinct. (There are many double forms in cultivation in which the stamens have changed into petals leaving but few or no stamens.) Figs. 335 to 342 29

28b Stamens usually arising around or above the ovary, sepals usually on the edge of a cup-like receptacle. Figs. 343 to 346. 36

29a Aquatic herbs; carpels 3 or more, petals large; usually large floating peltate leaves. Water Lily Family, NYMPHAEACEAE

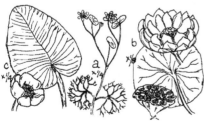

Figure 335

Fig.335. a, <u>Cabomba caroliniana</u> A. Gray, Cabomba; b, <u>Nelumbo lutea</u> (Willd.), American Lotus; c, <u>Nymphaea advena</u> Soland, Cow Lily.

This and the genus <u>Castalia</u> have the carpels united in a compound pistil. Many exotic water lilies with beautifully tinted flowers are available for lily pools.

29b Growing on land or in marshes (a few species of
Ranunculaceae submerged), stamens many; sepals distinct.
Figs. 336 to 342. .30

30a Receptacle hollow, containing many carpels and their achenes,
roughly appearing as a compound ovary. Aromatic shrubs, with
opposite entire leaves.   Calycanthus Family, CALYCANTHACEAE

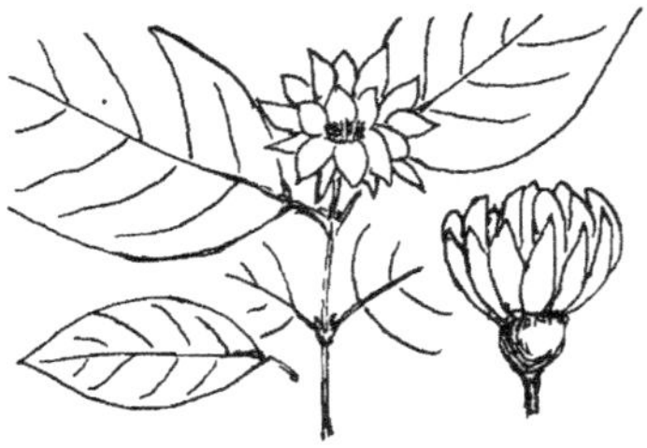

Fig.336. a, <u>Calycanthus floridus</u>
L., Hairy Strawberry Shrub.

So-called because of the odor
of strawberries given off by the
dark purplish-red flowers. A native of southeastern United States
but much planted as an ornamental.

Figure 336

30b Receptacle not hollow. Leaves almost always alternate.
Figs. 337 to 342. .31

31a Climbing vines with
simple alternate leaves and
small dioecious flowers.
Moonseed Family, MENISPERMACEAE

Fig.337. <u>Menispermum cana-
dense</u> L., Canada Moonseed.

Flowers white, drupes
bluish-black resembling a
bunch of small grapes. Most
of the members of the family
are tropical.

Figure 337

31b Not vines with simple leaves, or if so, then the flowers are
perfect. Figs. 338 to 342. 32

32a Trees and shrubs with large entire (rarely lobed) alternate
leaves; sepals 3. Figs. 338 and 339. 33

32b Not as in 32a. Figs. 340 to 342 34

33a Sepals (3) and petals (6) meeting at their edges in the bud
(valvate) flowers not showy; fruit large, fleshy elongated
berries.   Custard Apple Family, ANONACEAE

Fig.338. <u>Asimina triloba</u> Dunal, Common Papaw.

The inter-dependence of plants and animals
is well illustrated here. The Zebra butterfly,
one of our most attractive swallow tails, feeds
in its larval state only on the Papaw. To look
for it in regions where Papaw does not grow is
a waste of time.

Figure 338

110

**33b Sepals (3) and petals (6 to 12) overlapping in the bud
(imbricate); flowers fragrant and showy; fruit cone-like.**
                              Magnolia Family, MAGNOLIACEAE

Fig.339. a, <u>Liriodendron
tulipifera</u> L., Tulip-tree;
b, <u>Magnolia virginiana</u> L.,
Sweetbay.

These plants naturally belong to the southern states,
but the Tulip-tree and a few
species of magnolias can be
raised in the north if given a
bit of extra care.

Figure 339

**34a Carpels usually more than 1; sepals 3-15 overlapping in the
bud; petal occasionally 0 but usually 3 to many; fruit an
achene, follicle or berry; anthers not opening by valves.**
                              Crowfoot Family, RANUNCULACEAE

Fig.340. a, <u>Delphinium tricorne</u>
Michx., Dwarf Larkspur; b, <u>Ranun-
culus acris</u> L., Meadow Buttercup.
Often cultivated, sometimes very
double. c, <u>Actaea rubra</u> (Ait.),
Red Baneberry.

Other common examples: Peony,
Clematis, Anemone, and Meadow Rue.
All of which are favorite garden
ornamentals.

Figure 340

34b Carpels only 1. Figs. 341 and 342 35

**35a Sepals more than 2; fruit a berry or capsule; anthers open-
ing by valves.**
                              Barberry Family, BERBERIDACEAE

Fig.341. a, <u>Berberis vulgaris</u> L.,
European Barberry. Outlawed
throughout the wheat belt as it
is the alternating host of Black
Stem Rust of wheat. b, <u>Podo-
phyllum peltatum</u> L., May Apple.

Often very abundant in low
woods. The fruit is edible. When
ripe it has a very characteristic
flavor.

Figure 341

**35b Sepals 2; climbing herbs with tubers at roots or on the
vines.**
                              Basella Family, BASELLACEAE

Figure 342

Fig.342. <u>Boussingaultia</u> <u>baseloides</u> H. B. K., Madeira-Vine.

A rapid-growing vine with white flowers and little tubers in axil of leaves. Native of tropical America, but running wild in southern U. S. Often planted as an ornamental vine.

36a Fruit a legume (pea-like pod); flowers usually sweet pea-shaped (a few are regular); leaves usually compound.
Pea Family, LEGUMINOSAE

Figure 343

Fig.343. <u>Vicia</u> <u>micrantha</u> Nutt., Small-flowered Vetch; b, <u>Cassia</u> <u>chamae-crista</u> L., Partridge Pea; c, <u>Trifolium</u> <u>repens</u> L., White Clover.

This family furnishes some highly important foods for man and beast.

Common examples: Peas, Beans, Peanuts, Alfalfa, and many beautiful and valuable trees.

36b Not as in 36a. Figs. 344 to 346 37

37a Herbs, with perfectly symmetrical flowers (sepals, petals and carpels of same number and stamens of same or double number); leaves without stipules; fruit a follicle.
Orpine Family, CRASSULACEAE

Figure 344

Fig.344. <u>Sedum</u> <u>purpureum</u> L., Live-for-ever.

.This species introduced from Europe is common in cultivation and as an escape.

37b Not as in 37a. Figs. 345 and 346. 38

38a Regular flowers with many stamens (rarely few) and the 5 petals often notched; leaves with stipules; seeds with no endosperm. (Many cultivated forms are double as the result of stamens turning into petals. Such forms may have few or no stamens).
Rose Family, ROSACEAE

Figure 345

Fig.345. a, Geum canadense Jacq., White Avens; b, Prunus nigra Ait., Canada Plum; c, Rosa virginiana Mill., Wild Rose.

A large and highly important family for beauty and use.

Common examples: Strawberries, Raspberries, Blackberries, Plums, Peach, Cherries, Apples, Quinces, Roses, and Spirea.

38b   Stamens seldom more than 10, usually less; seeds with endosperm; leaves often without stipules.
Saxifrage Family, SAXIFRAGACEAE

Figure 346

Fig.346. a, Heuchera hispida Pursh., Rough Alum-root; b, Ribes vulgare Lam., Common Garden Currant.

Common examples: Deutzias, Syringas, Currants, and Gooseberries.

38c   Shrubs and trees with simple alternate leaves and fruit a woody capsule. (Often without petals). See Fig. 311.
Witch-Hazel Family, HAMAMELIDACEAE

39a   Stamens many (more than 10 and more than twice the sepals or calyx lobes). Figs. 347 to 357 40

39b   Stamens 10 or less. (Not more than twice the petals). Figs. 358 to 402. 50

40a   Ovary raised above corolla by a stalk; corolla with a fringed crown. Vines with tendrils, or erect herbs. Fruit a berry with many seeds.   Passion Flower Family, PASSIFLORACEAE

Figure 347

Fig.347. Passiflora incarnata L., Passion Flower.

Flowers are white or lavender with pink or purple crown. Native throughout the South.

40b   Ovary sessile; flowers without a crown; no tendrils. Figs. 348 to 357. 41

41a Sepals 2; herbs. Figs. 348 to 350 42

41b Sepals more than 2. Figs. 351 to 357. 44

42a Flowers perfect. Figs. 349 and 350. 43

42b Flowers with stamens or pistils only. Monoecious. Succu-
     lent tender herbs raised as house plants and in greenhouse.
                                    Begonia Family, BEGONIACEAE

Figure 348

Fig.348. a, <u>Begonia</u> <u>semperflorens</u>
L. & O.; b, <u>Begonia</u> <u>tuberhy-</u>
<u>brida</u> Voss.

Many important house plants belong to this family, all falling
in the one genus, <u>Begonia</u>, which
is also the common name. The
hybrid Tuberous-Rooted Begonias
are among the most showy species.

43a Leaves thickened, succulent, entire (rarely 5 sepals).
                                    Purslane Family, PORTULACACEAE

Figure 349

Fig.349. a, <u>Portulaca</u> <u>grandiflora</u>
Hook., Rose Moss. Flowers pink,
red, yellow, white; often double;
cultivated. Introduced from
South America. b, <u>Talinum</u>
<u>calysinum</u> Engelm., Large-flowered
Talinum.

Many of the members of this family
are xerophytes (belong naturally in
regions of scanty rainfall).

43b Leaves often deeply cut or lobed, their tips often with
     spines. Juice milky or colored. Petals in pairs, 4-12.
     Flowers usually showy.   Poppy Family, PAPAVERACEAE

Figure 351

Fig.350. a, <u>Papaver</u> rhoeas L.,
Corn Poppy. Flowers scarlet
with dark center; b, <u>Sangui-</u>
<u>naria</u> canadensis, L. Blood-
root. The sepals drop when
the flower opens.

The Oriental poppies are
perhaps the most showy of all
the many species of poppies.
Opium is made from the sap of
one species.

44a Leaves with transparent or black dots. Stamens usually
     united in groups of 3's or 5's.
                              St. John's-wort Family, HYPERICACEAE

114

Figure 351

Fig.351. <u>Hypericum prolificum</u> L., Shrubby St. Johns-wort.

The flowers are usually yellow. The plants may be herbs or shrubs or sometimes small trees.

44b Leaves and stamens not as in 44a. Figs. 352 to 357. . . .45

45a Stamens united in one or a few large groups, sepals meeting at their edges. Figs. 352 and 353. 46

45b Stamens separate. Sepals overlapping in the bud. Figs. 354 to 357. 47

46a Stamens united in a central column surrounding the pistil (Fig. c).   Mallow Family, MALVACEAE

Figure 352

Fig.352. a, <u>Hibiscus trinonum</u> L., Flower-of-an-Hour; b, <u>Malva rotundifolia</u> L., Low Mallow.

Common examples: Cotton, Hibiscus, Hollyhock, and Indian Mallow (a most persistent weed).

46b Trees (in our region) with stamens in groups of five to ten each.   Linden Family, TILIACEAE

Figure 353

Fig.353. <u>Tilia glabra</u> Vent., Basswood.

The wood is valued for combining whiteness, light weight, and fine grain. It is much used in cabinet work.

47a Leaves hollow; pitcher, or trumpet shaped; herbs; in bogs.   Pitcher Plant Family, SARRACENIACEAE

Figure 354

Fig.354. <u>Sarracenia</u> <u>purpurea</u> L., Pitcher Plant.

These plants are always interesting. <u>Sarracenia</u> <u>flava</u> L. commonly known as "Trumpets" grows abundantly in bogs of our southeastern states. The yellow and red leaves sometimes attain a height of three feet and are very conspicuous to man and doubtless also to the insects they trap.

47b Not as in 47a. Figs. 355 to 357 48

48a Flowers not symmetrical. Figs. 356 and 357. 49

Figure 355

48b Flowers symmetrical, leaves simple, almost always entire; sepals 3, or sometimes with an additional 2 small outer ones.
Rock-rose Family, CISTACEAE

Fig.355. a, <u>Helianthemum</u> <u>canadense</u> Michx., Rock-rose, flowers bright yellow; b, <u>Hudsonia</u> <u>ericoides</u> L., American Heath.

Sandy soil in pine barrens suits it best.

49a Calyx persistent; open in bud; sepals and petals irregular, 4-8.
Mignonette Family, RESEDACEAE

Figure 356

Fig.356. <u>Reseda</u> <u>lutea</u> L., Yellow Cut-leaved Mignonette.

The garden mignonette (<u>Reseda</u> <u>ordorata</u> L.) was an old time favorite largely because of its fragrance. Its leaves are entire or sometimes 3 lobed.

49b Sepals usually falling off, 4-8; petals 4; sap watery; leaves usually palmately compound.   Caper Family, CAPPARIDACEAE

Figure 357

Fig.357. <u>Polanisia</u> <u>graveolens</u> Raf., Clammy-weed.

Common along sandy shores. The viscid pubescens of the leaves accounts for the common name.

50a Stamens 6 (rarely less); petals 4; sepals 2 or 4. Figs. 358 to 360. 51

50b Not as in 50a. Figs. 361 to 402 53

51a Stamens united in 2 sets of 3; flowers irregular; sepals 2, scale-like.   Fumitory Family, FUMARIACEAE

Figure 358

Fig.358. a, <u>Dicentra</u> <u>cucullaria</u> (L.), Dutchman's Breeches; b, <u>Corydalis</u> <u>aurea</u>, Willd. Golden Corydalis.

This is only a small family. The old-fashioned favorite "Bleeding Heart" belongs here.

51b Stamens not united; flowers regular; sepals 4. Figs. 359 and 360 52

52a Stamens alike; leaves usually palmately compound; capsule 1-celled.   Caper Family, CAPPARIDACEAE

Figure 359

Fig.359. <u>Cleome</u> <u>spinosa</u> L., Spider-flower.

Though this is only a weed introduced from tropical America, it is often planted as an ornamental garden plant.

52b Stamens in two whorls, 4 long and 2 short (rarely only 2 or 4); capsule 2-celled.   Mustard Family, CRUCIFERAE

Figure 360

Fig.360. a, <u>Capsella</u> <u>bursa-pastoris</u> (L.), Shepherd's Purse; b, <u>Brassica</u> <u>juncea</u> (L.), Indian Mustard; c, typical mustard flower.

Common examples: Turnip, Rape, Kohlrabi, Cauliflower, Cabbage, Horse Radish, Honesty, and Radish.

117

53a Stamens as many as the petals with a
stamen in front of each petal. Fig.
361a. 54

Figure 361

53b Stamens between the petals (alternating) or more numerous. Fig. 361b . . 57

54a Calyx of 2 sepals; flowers perfect.

Purslane Family, PORTULACACEAE

Figure 362

Fig.362. Claytonia virginica L.,
Spring Beauty.

This plain-looking little plant
literally carpets the woods throughout
much of the east and south in early
spring. The flowers are white with a
faint pinkish tint.

54b Calyx with more than 2 sepals; fruit a drupe, berry or
capsule. Figs. 363 to 365. 55

Figure 363

55a Petals 6 or more; petals and sepals both
imbricated in the bud. Ovary 1-celled.

Barberry Family, BERBERIDACEAE

x ¼

Fig.363. Jeffersonia diphyllum (L.), Twin Leaf.

The genus name was given in honor of Thomas
Jefferson; the species name refers to the divided
leaves. The flowers are white.

55b Petals and stamens only 4 or 5; ovary 2-4 celled. Figs.
364 and 365 56

56a Tendril-climbing woody vines, rarely shrubs; petals falling
very early, calyx minute; fruit a berry.

Grape Family, VITACEAE

Figure 364

Fig.364. a, Psedera quinquefolia
Gr., Virginia Creeper, a highly
attractive non-poisonous "Ivy";
b, Vitis vulpina L., River Grape.

Wild grapes are widely distributed. From them many of our best
cultivated varieties have been
developed.

118

56b Shrubs or small trees, rarely vines; fruit a drupe or capsule; calyx plainly 4 or 5-parted; petals sometimes wanting.
Buckthorn Family, RHAMNACEAE

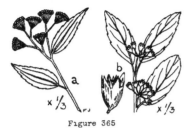

Fig.365. a, Ceanothus americanus
L., New Jersey Tea. The small
white flowers are attractive.
b, Rhamnus caroliniana Walt.,
Carolina Buckthorn.

The flowers of the New Jersey Tea
are white and very soft. They
attract large numbers of insects so
that the insect collector does well
to know this plant.

Figure 365

57a Ovary with only 1 cell. Figs. 366 to 374. 58

57b Ovary with 2 or more cells. Figs. 375 to 402. 65

58a Ovules or seeds attached to walls of
ovary (parietal placenta). Fig. 366a . . 59

58b Ovules or seeds attached at base or
center of ovary (central placenta). Fig.
366b. 64

Figure 366

58c Usually but one ovule in a one-celled ovary (rarely more
than 1-cell but then with one ovule to each cell). Trees or
shrubs with resinous bark or milky sap.
Cashew Family, ANACARDIACEAE

Fig.367. a, Rhus toxicodendron L.,
Poison Ivy; b, Rhus glabra L.,
Smooth Sumac.

It is of vital importance for
every nature lover to recognize
Poison Ivy.

Figure 367

59a Stamens with filaments united. See Fig. 352.
Mallow Family, MALVACEAE

59b Stamens on separate filaments. Figs. 368 to 372 60

60a Fertile stamens 5; with numerous sterile stamens
(staminodia) at base of each petal.
Grass-of-Parnassus Family, PARNASSIACEAE

119

Figure 368

Fig.368. <u>Parnassia</u> <u>caroliniana</u> Michx., Grass-of-Parnassus.

In bogs and moist soil. Flowers greenish white.

60b All stamens fertile. Figs. 369 to 372 61

61a Leaves with gland-tipped sticky hairs for catching insects.
                      Sundew Family, DROSERACEAE

Figure 369

Fig.369. <u>Drosera</u> <u>rotundifolia</u> L., Round-leaved Sundew.

In bogs; widely distributed. These small fragile plants are likely to prove disappointing to one who has studied about them, when they are seen, for the first time. The insects they catch are usually tiny ones. There are several species.

61b Leaves not for catching insects. Figs. 370 to 372 62

Figure 370

62a Leaves with black or transparent
     dots; entire or scale-like.
      St. John's-wort Family, HYPERICACEAE

Fig.370. a, <u>Triadenum</u> <u>virginicum</u> L., Marsh St.John's-wort. Flowers reddish-purple; stamens in 3 sets of 3 each; b, <u>Sarothra</u> <u>gentianoides</u> L., Orange Grass.

Grows in sandy soil.

62b Leaves not dotted. Figs. 371 and 372. 63

Figure 371

63a Corolla irregular; flowers pansy-
      shaped.   Violet Family, VIOLACEAE

Fig.371. a, <u>Viola</u> <u>pedata</u> L., Bird's-foot Violet; b, <u>Viola</u> <u>striata</u> Ait., Pale Violet.

Violets are favorites everywhere. The pansy belongs to this same family.

63b Corolla regular; sepals and petals 3 or 5.
$\qquad\qquad\qquad\qquad$ **Rock-rose Family, CISTACEAE**

Figure 372

Fig.372. Lechea tenuifolia Michx., Narrow-
$\quad$ leaved Pin-weed.

$\quad$ The flowers are a purplish-red. The
species is widely scattered east of the
Missouri River.

**64a Herbs with opposite or whorled, usually entire leaves; stems
usually swollen at the joints.   Pink Family, CARYOPHYLLACEAE**

Figure 373

Fig.373. a, Cerastium nutans Raf.,
$\quad$ Nodding Chickweed; b, Saponaria
$\quad$ officinalis L., Bouncing Bet.

$\quad$ This rather large family includes the
Carnation, Sweet William, Baby's Breath,
and Garden Pinks.

Figure 374

**64b Shrubs with alternate leaves, usually scale-
like.**

$\qquad\qquad$ **Tamarisk Family, TAMARICACEAE**

Fig.374. Tamarix gallica L.

$\quad$ Though frequently planted, these scraggly, open
shrubs are curious rather than attractive. The
flowers are pink.

**65a Stamens united with each other and with the thickened stigma
arising from the two ovaries.   Milkweed Family, ASCLEPIADACEAE**

Figure 375

Fig.375. a, Asclepias
$\quad$ incarnata L., Swamp Milk-
$\quad$ weed; b, Acerates viridi-
$\quad$ flora (Raf.), Green Milk-
$\quad$ weed.

$\quad$ There are many very attrac-
tively marked and colored
milkweeds. They are widely
distributed and vary much in
size.

65b Stamens not as in 65a. Figs. 376 to 402 66

66a Flowers irregular (bilaterally symmetrical). Figs. 376 to
379 67

66b Flowers regular (radially symmetrical). Figs. 380 to
402 69

67a Trees or shrubs; leaves palmately compound, opposite.
                              Soapberry Family, SAPINDACEAE

Fig.376. <u>Aesculus</u> <u>glabra</u> Willd., Ohio Buckeye.

This family includes a number of foreign plants cultivated as ornamentals. Buckeyes and Horse-chestnuts are widely distributed. There are several species, some with red flowers.

Figure 376

67b Herbs; leaves simple. Figs. 377 to 379. 68

68a Ovary 5-celled; stems soft, succulent, stamens 5-10; one
sepal prolonged back into nectar sac or spur.
                              Balsam Family, BALSAMINACEAE

Fig.377. <u>Impatiens</u> <u>biflora</u> Walt., Wild Touch-me-not. Flowers vermilion. The Pale Touch-me-not is a larger plant with pale yellow flowers. It is the seed pods (b) that may "not-be-touched" for they "explode" with the slightest irritation.

Figure 377

68b Ovary 3 celled; stamens 8, leaves peltate or palmately
divided.   Nasturtium Family, TROPAEOLACEAE

Fig.378. <u>Tropaeolum</u> <u>majus</u> L., Garden Nasturtium.

This favorite flower→garden ornamental is a native of South America. The stems, seeds and buds are sometimes used in pickles for their flavor.

·Figure 378

68c Ovary 2-celled; stamens 6-8; leaves simple, entire, with
stipules.   Milkwort Family, POLYGALACEAE

Fig.379. a, <u>Polygala viridescens</u> L., Purple
Milkwort; b, <u>Polygala polygama</u> Walt
Racemed Milkwort.

The family has about 1000 species, many of
which are confined to the tropics.

Figure 379

69a Stamens same number as the petals or twice as many. Figs. 380 to 398. 70

69b Stamens not as In 69a. Figs. 399 to 402 89

70a Ovules and usually the seeds more than 2 in each cavity of the ovary. Figs. 393 to 398. 83

70b Ovules or seeds not more than 2 in each cavity. Figs. 380 to 392. 71

71a Trees or shrubs. Figs. 380 to 387 72

71b Herbaceous plants. Figs. 388 to 392 79

72a Leaves simple. Figs. 380 to 384 73

72b Leaves compound. Figs. 385 to 387 . . . . .77´

73a Leaves opposite; lobed and palmately-veined or pinnately-compound; no stipules. Fruit splitting into two-winged samaras.   Maple Family, ACERACEAE

Fig.380. <u>Acer platanoides</u> L., Norway Maple.

Sugar-making from maple sap was once a
highly important early spring industry but
is losing its importance. Maple trees
furnish some fine lumber.

Figure 380

73b Leaves pinnately veined. Figs. 381 to 384 74

74a Leaves opposite; woody vines, shrubs or small trees. Staff-tree Family, CELASTRACEAE

Fig.381. <u>Evonymus atropurpureus</u> Jacq.,
Wahoo.

The salmon-pink fruit which upon opening
displays its vermilion seeds never fails to
attract attention.

Figure 381

74b Leaves alternate 75

75a Climbing woody vines.   **Staff-tree Family, CELASTRACEAE**

Figure 382

Fig.382. <u>Celastrus</u> <u>scandens</u> L., Bitter-
 sweet.

Its fruit is much prized for winter
decoration. In color it is much like the
Wahoo.

75b Woody plants, not climbing. Figs. 383 and 384 76

Figure 383

**76a Flowers small, in racemes. Leaves
 thick, entire. Fruit dry.**
          Cyrilla Family, CYRILLACEAE

Fig.383. <u>Cyrilla</u> <u>racemiflora</u> L., Leather-
 wood.

This small family of trees and shrubs belongs in the South. The species here used as
an example grows in wet places.

Figure 384

**76b Flowers solitary or clustered in the
 axils. Leaves often leathery, simple;
 fruit a berry-like drupe with several hard
 seeds.**   **Holly Family, AQUIFOLIACEAE**

Fig.384. <u>Nemopanthus</u> <u>mucronata</u> (L.), Mountain
 Holly.

It is found in swamps. It is not evergreen
as most of the other members of the family.

**77a Leaves with glandular punctations (translucent dots).
 Pistils sometimes 1–5, distinct.**   **Rue Family, RUTACEAE**

Figure 385

Fig.385. a, <u>Ptelea</u> <u>trifoliata</u>
 L., Hoptree; b, <u>Zanthoxylum</u>
 <u>americanum</u> Mill., Prickly Ash.

The Hoptree, a shrub or small
tree, has very characteristic
fruit which has won for it the
name "Wafer-Ash". Its range is
throughout much of the eastern
half of the U.S.

124

77b Leaves not punctate. Figs. 386 and 387. 78

78a Fruit (in our one species) a winged samara. An open-growing
 tree with thick branches and long pinnately-compound leaves.
                        Ailanthus Family, SIMARUBACEAE

Figure 386

Fig.386. Ailanthus altissima Swingle,
   Tree of Heaven.

   This tree is a native of China. It
grows rapidly and its leaves have an un-
pleasant odor. It sprouts vigorously
and at considerable distances from the
parent tree.

78b Fruit of many forms but not a samara.
                        Soapberry Family, SAPINDACEAE

Figure 387

Fig.387. Sapindus drummondii H. & A.;
   Soapberry.

   This tree may attain a height of 50
feet. It belongs to the South and
West.

79a Flowers imperfect; monoecious or dioecious; sap usually
 acrid or milky.   Spurge Family, EUPHORBIACEAE

Figure 388

Fig.388. a, Croton monanthogynus Michx.,
   Single Fruited Croton; b, Croton
   glandulosa L. Glandular Croton.

   This is a large important family.
With many species the maturing ovary is
so large and so suspended on a slender
stem that it hangs out of the flower in
a very characteristic way.

   Common examples: Poinsettia, Castor-
oil Plant, Para Rubber Tree.

79b Flowers perfect and regular. Figs. 389 to 392 80

80a Sepals and carpels (cells of the ovary) of the same number.
 Figs. 389 and 390 81

80b Twice as many carpels as sepals. Figs. 391 and 392. . . .82

81a One ovule to each carpel; ovary 2-3 celled.
                        False Mermaid Family, LIMNANTHACEAE

125

Fig.389. <u>Floerkea</u> <u>proserpinacoides</u> Willd., False Mermaid.

Flowers red, pink or white. The species used here grows in marshes and other wet places.

Figure 389

81b One or two ovules to each carpel; ovary 5-celled, splitting at maturity; stamens with versatile anthers.
                        Geranium Family, GERANIACEAE

Fig.390. a, <u>Geranium</u> <u>maculatum</u> L., Wild Crane's Bill; b, <u>Erodium</u> <u>circutarium</u> (L.), Red-stem Filaree.

The showy cultivated "geraniums" belong to this family, but to the genus <u>Pelargonium</u> rather than <u>Geranium</u>.

Figure 390

82a Leaves pinnately compound.   Caltrop Family, ZYGOPHYLLACEAE

Fig.391. <u>Kallstroemia</u> <u>intermedia</u> Rydb.; Greater Caltrop.

The flowers are yellow and the plants hairy.

Figure 391

82b Leaves simple, stipules small or none, styles 2-5.
                        Flax Family, LINACEAE

Fig.392. a, <u>Linum</u> <u>usitatissimum</u> L., Flax.

This important plant is widely cultivated. Its fibers produce linen and from its seed comes linseed oil.

Figure 392

126

83a   Leaves simple. Figs. 393 to 396 84

83b   Leaves compound. Figs. 397 and 398. 88

84a   Leaves simple, opposite, with stipules between them; small plants growing in marshes.   Waterwort Family, ELATINACEAE

Fig.393. Elatine triandra Schk., Waterwort.

    This is a mid-west and western plant that lives, as its name indicates, in lakes and such.

Figure 393

84b   Leaves alternate, or if opposite then without stipules. Figs. 394 to 398. 85

85a   Pistil with 2 to 5 styles. 87

85b   Pistil with but one style. Figs. 394 and 395. 86

86a   Stamens arising from the calyx; leaves usually opposite.
                           Loosestrife Family, LYTHRACEAE

Fig.394. Lythrum alatum Pursh., Wing-angled Loosestrife.

    It grows in low damp ground; its flowers are purple. The very showy shrub, Crape-Myrtle, of our southern states, belongs in this family.

Figure 394

86b   Stamens not attached to the calyx.   Heath Family, ERICACEAE

Fig.395. a, Monotropa uniflora L., Indian Pipe; b, Pyrola secunda L., One-sided Wintergreen.

    The family is very important in the decorative plants both native and cultivated, that belongs to it, such as the Heaths, Heather, Laurels, Rhododendrons, and Azaleas.

Figure 395

87a   Stamens arising from the calyx. Fig. 395.
                              Heath Family, ERICACEAE

87b   Stamens not attached to calyx; nodes of stems usually swollen.   Pink Family, CARYOPHYLLACEAE

Figure 396

Fig.396. <u>Silene noctiflora</u> L., Night-flower-
ing Catchfly.

This family while producing some valued
ornamentals, also has many serious weeds among
its members.

Figure 397

**88a Herbs with sour sap; ovary-5 celled;
stamens 10-15; leaves usually with 3
obcordate leaflets.
Wood Sorrel Family, OXALIDACEAE**

Fig.397. <u>Oxalis corniculata</u> (L.), Yellow
Wood-sorrel.

These plants are often called "Sheep-
sorrel" but that name should be reserved for
<u>Rumex acetosella</u>.

**88b Shrubs or trees; carpels usually 3; fruit an inflated
capsule.   Bladder-nut Family, STAPHYLEACEAE**

Figure 398

Fig.398. <u>Staphylea trifolia</u> L.,
American Bladder-nut.

This is a small family with several
species being raised for ornament. The
inflated fruit never fails to attract
attention.

89a Herbaceous plants. Figs. 399 and 400. 90

89b Shrubs or trees. Figs. 401 and 402. 91

**90a Sepals and petals 4; stamens 6 or less; fruit a silique or
silicle.   Mustard Family, CRUCIFERAE**

Figure 399

Fig.399. a, <u>Sisymbrium officinale</u>
L., Hedge Mustard; b, <u>Cardamine
douglassii</u> (Torr.), Purple Cress.

The cross-shaped, 4-petaled flowers
are characteristic of this important
family as are also the seed pods.

90b Sepals and petals 5.   St. John's-wort Family, HYPERICACEAE

Figure 400

Fig.400. <u>Hypericum</u> <u>mutilum</u> L., Dwarf St.
John's-wort.

Most of the members of the family are
characterized by their many stamens; this
species is one of the exceptions.

91a Petals 4, stamens fewer.   Olive Family, OLEACEAE

Figure 401

Fig.401. a, <u>Ligustrum</u> <u>vulgare</u>
L., Privet; b, <u>Chionanthus</u>
<u>virginica</u> L., Fringe-tree.

As the family name indi-
cates, the Olive belongs here.
Other important members of the
family are Ash, furnishing
excellent wood for tool-making,
and Lilac and Jasmine.

**91b With more stamens than petals.
Maple Family, ACERACEAE**

Figure 402

Fig.402. <u>Acer</u> <u>spicatum</u> Lam., Mountain
Maple.

The family boasts but two genera but
many species of widely distributed trees
and shrubs. Maples are important for
ornament, their wood and their sugar.

**92a Herbaceous vines, bearing tendrils.
Gourd Family, CUCURBITACEAE**

Figure 403

Fig.403. <u>Sicyos</u> <u>angulatus</u> L., Star
Cucumber.

This important family includes many
food plants; Pumpkins, Squashes, Gourds,
Watermelons, Muskmelon, Cucumbers, and
some ornamental vines.

92b Exotic, usually evergreen aromatic shrubs or trees; sepals and petals 4-5, stamens many, ovary 1 to many-celled.
Myrtle Family, MYRTACEAE

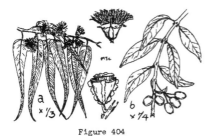

Figure 404

Fig.404. a, <u>Eucalyptus</u> sp.; b, <u>Eugenia myrtifolia</u> Sims., Australian Brush-Cherry.

This important family belongs to Australia and the tropics. It yields valuable lumber oils, gums, cloves, alspice and many other commercial products.

92c Not as in 92a or 92b. Figs. 405 to 417. 93

93a But one seed or ovule in each cell of ovary. Figs. 405 to 410. 94

93b More than one seed or ovule in each cell of the ovary. Figs. 411 to 417. .99

94a With 2, 4, or 8 stamens. Figs. 405 to 407 95

94b With 5 or 10 stamens. Figs. 408 to 410. 97

95a Shrubs and trees with drupe-like fruit and single style and stigma.   Dogwood Family, CORNACEAE

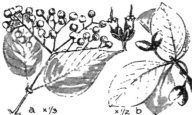

Figure 405

Fig.405. a, <u>Cornus asperifolia</u> Michx., Rough-leaved Dogwood; b, <u>Nyssa biflora</u> Walt., Swamp Black Gum.

The family consists mostly of shrubs and trees though an occasional herb figures in it. There are some 10 genera in all but <u>Cornus</u> is the most important.

95b Herbs. Figs. 406 and 407. 96

Figure 406

96a Styles 4 (sometimes with 4 sessile stigmas).
Water-milfoil Family, HALORAGIDACEAE

Fig.406. <u>Myriophyllum spicatum</u> L., Spiked Water-milfoil.

These water plants play an important part in our watercourses in fish and game culture. Some species are seen in indoor aquaria.

96b With but one style; stigma 2 to 4-branched.
                    Evening-Primrose Family, ONAGRACEAE

Figure 407

Fig.407. *Gaura biennis* L., Biennial Gaura.

Tropical America and New Zealand brings us the Fuchsia, several species of which are common ornamentals. They belong to this family.

97a Fruit fleshy. Figs. 409 and 410 98

97b Fruit dry when ripe; herbs; flowers small, generally in simple or compound umbels; petals 5; stamens 5; leaves alternate and usually compound.   Carrot Family, UMBELLIFERAE

Figure 408

Fig.408. a, *Pastinaca sativa* L., Parsnip; b, *Eryngium yuccaefolium* Mich., Rattlesnake-master.

This large and distinctly marked family includes many favorite ornamentals as well as some well-known food plants, such as Carrot, Parsley, and Celery. Herbs for seasoning furnished by the family include Dill, Cumin, Coriander, Lovage, Anise, Myrrh, and Caraway. Several highly poisonous plants also belong here, the Poison-Hemlock being an outstanding example.

98a Leaves simple; with no prickles. Trees or shrubs. Fruit a pome.   Rose Family (in part), ROSACEAE

Figure 409

Fig.409. *Crataegus punctata* Jacq., Dotted Thorn.

This is an exceptionally large family. The genus *Crataegus* in itself has more than a thousand species.

98b Leaves compound; or if simple, with prickles. Herbs, shrubs, trees. Fruit a drupe or berry.
                    Ginseng Family, ARALIACEAE

131

Fig.410. <u>Aralia nudicaulis</u> L.,
Wild Sarsaparilla.

The Ginsengs, important as
drugs, belong to this family and
are often raised on a large
scale.

Figure 410

**99a Spiny, fleshy plants; stems often jointed; leaves absent or
small; numerous petals and sepals; stamens on a hypanthium.**
Cactus Family, CACTACEAE

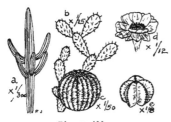

Fig.411. a, <u>Carnegiea gigantea</u>
Suwarro, Giant Cactus, the
largest known cactus; may attain
a height of 40 feet; b, <u>Opuntia
engelmannii</u> S-D.; c, <u>Echinocactus
grusonii</u> Hild, Golden Cactus;
d, typical cactus flower;
e, <u>Astrophytum myriostigma</u>,
Bishop's Cap.

Figure 411

99b Not as in 99a. Figs. 412 to 417. 100

100a Ovary with but one cell. Figs. 412 to 414. 101

100b Ovary with 2 or more cells. Figs. 415 to 417 103

**101a Sepals or calyx lobes 2; smooth herbs with fleshy entire
leaves.   Purslane Family, PORTULACACEAE**

Fig.412. <u>Portulaca oleraceae</u> L.,
Purslane.

Very common in gardens. Being a
xerophyte, it can stand much more
abuse than most of its competitors.

Figure 412

**101b Sepals or calyx lobes more than 2. Figs. 413 and 414
. . . . 102**

**102a Erect or climbing herbs, with stinging or glandular hairs;
stamens many; petals 5 or sometimes appearing as 10.**
Loasa Family, LOASACEAE

Figure 413

Fig.413. a, <u>Mentzelia</u> <u>albicau-</u><u>lis</u> Dougl., White-stemmed Mentzelia; b, <u>Nuttallia</u> <u>decapetala</u> (Pursh), Prairie Lily.

This family belongs principally to the western part of our country. The greater number of species belong in South America.

102b Shrubs with small solitary or racemed flowers. Petals or stamens 4 or 5.   Saxifrage Family, SAXIFRAGACEAE

Figure 414

Fig.414. <u>Ribes gracile</u> Pursh., Missouri Gooseberry.

Gooseberries and Currants are western hemisphere plants. Our cultivated forms have been bred up from the native stock. The Golden Currant is an ornamental shrub.

Figure 415

103a Anthers opening by pores at their tip. Leaves opposite with 3 to 9 nerves. Meadow-beauty Family, MELASTOMACEAE

Fig.415. <u>Rhexia</u> <u>virginica</u> L., Meadow-beauty.

This large family is pretty much confined to the tropics. Some of these tropical species may be found in hot-houses.

103b Anthers opening along their sides; stamens arising from the calyx. Figs. 416 and 417 104

Figure 416

104a Stamens 4 or 8; styles 1; base of calyx usually forming an elongated tube. Evening-Primrose Family, ONAGRACEAE

Fig.416. <u>Oenothera</u> <u>biennis</u> L., Common Evening-Primrose.

If one wishes to see flowers open naturally, this family and the above species makes an excellent example. The whole process, once it has started, takes but a few minutes.

133

Figure 417

104b Styles 2 to 5; stamens 8 to many.
Saxifrage Family, SAXIFRAGACEAE

Fig.417. <u>Philadelphus</u> <u>cornarius</u>, Mock Orange.

This species can be told from the other Syringas by the fragrant odor of its flowers.

105a Calyx arising below the ovary (or surrounding its base). (Ovary superior). Fig. 418a. 113

105b Calyx arising above the ovary. (Ovary inferior). Fig. 418b. 106

Figure 418

106a Flowers of one or more kinds crowded in heads with one or more rings of bracts beneath; the 5 anthers united at their sides to form a tube surrounding the style (when present).
Composite Family, COMPOSITAE

Figure 419

Fig.419. a, <u>Taraxacum</u> <u>officinale</u> Weber, Common Dandelion; b, <u>Ambrosia</u> <u>artemisiaefolia</u> L., Common Ragweed; c, <u>Erigeron</u> <u>caespitosus</u> Nutt., Tufted Erigeron; d, <u>Liatris</u> <u>cylindracea</u> (Michx.), Cylindric Blazing Star.

This great family is readily distinguished by the characters given in the key. Many favorite ornamentals belong to it such as Sunflowers, Asters, Daisies, Marigolds, Strawflowers, Zinnias, Dahlias and Chrysanthemums. The family also furnishes a few food plants, Artichoke, Vegetable Oyster and Chicory.

106b Flowers not in dense-bracted (involucrate) heads. Figs. 420 to 426. 107

Figure 420

107a Herbaceous tendril-bearing vines. Fruit a pepo (pumpkin-like). Leaves palmately compound, lobed or veined.
Gourd Family, CUCURBITACEAE

Fig.420. <u>Cucumis</u> <u>sativis</u> L., Cucumber.

The flowers of many of the species are very conspicuous yet they are but little used for ornament. Gourds are prized for their decorative fruit.

134

107b Without tendrils. Figs. 421 to 426. 108

108a Stamens united by their anthers; flowers irregular usually
   in racemes, never in an involucrate head.
                                    Lobelia Family, LOBELIACEAE

Fig.421. <u>Lobelia</u> <u>cardinalis</u> L., Cardinal-
   flower.

   This is likely the most decorative species
of the family. It grows in damp places and is
very showy with its brilliant red flowers.

Figure 421

108b Stamens not united. Figs. 422 to 426. 109

109a Stamens arising from the walls of the corolla. Figs. 423
   to 426 110

109b Stamens not as in 109a; juice milky.
                                 Blue-bell Family, CAMPANULACEAE

Fig.422. a, <u>Campanula</u> <u>rotundi-</u>
   <u>folia</u> L., Blue Bells; b, <u>Campa-</u>
   <u>nula</u> <u>perfoliata</u> L., Venus' Look-
   ing-glass.

   Harebells, Canterbury Bells, and
Balloon-Flowers, among other favorite cultigens belong here. Blue is
the prevailing color of the
flowers.

Figure 422

110a Stamens 1 to 3 (rarely 4), fewer than the lobes of the
   corolla.   Valerian Family, VALERIANACEAE

Fig.423. <u>Valeriana</u> <u>officinalis</u>
   L., Garden Heliotrope.

   This European plant is sometimes found growing wild. It is
often seen in gardens.

Figure 423

110b Stamens 4-5; leaves opposite or whorled. Figs. 424 to 426.111

111a Ovary with but one cell. Flowers in dense involucrate
   heads.   Teasel Family, DIPSACACEAE

135

Figure 424

Fig.424. <u>Dipsacus sylvestris</u> .Huds., Common Teasel.

Another European plant introduced here as an ornamental and for use in weaving wool. The Pincushion Flower, a common garden favorite also belongs here.

111b Ovary with more than 1 cell. Figs. 425 and 426. 112

112a Leaves whorled or opposite and with stipules; petals usually 4.   Madder Family, RÚBIACEAE

Figure 425

Fig.425. a, <u>Houstonia coerulea</u> L., Bluets; b, <u>Galium aparine</u> L., Bed-straw.

From the lowly and despised Bed-straw to the prized Gardenia or the commercially important Coffee seems a far cry but all belong to this rather large family. The family also yields medical herbs and dye stuffs.

112b Leaves opposite, without stipules; often perfoliate; flowers frequently irregular. Honeysuckle Family,CAPRIFOLIACEAE

Figure 426

Fig.426. a, <u>Lonicera japonica</u> Thunb., Chinese Honeysuckle; b, <u>Sambucus canadensis</u> L., American Elder.

Honeysuckles may usually be told by the flowers and fruit growing in pairs. The leaves are often perfoliate. Buckbrush or Coral-berry prized by landscapists as a hedge shrub but a serious annoyance in farm pastures is a member of the family.

113a Stamens more in number than the lobes of the corolla. Figs. 427 to 436 114

113b Stamens not exceeding the number of corolla lobes. Figs. 437 to 472 122

114a Ovary with but one cell. Figs. 427 to 430 115

114b Ovary with more than one cell. Figs. 431 to 436 116

115a Ovules (seeds) all attached to one side of ovary (pod). Flowers often pea-shaped although sometimes regular. Leaves usually compound with stipules.   Pea Family, LEGUMINOSAE

Figure 427

Fig.427. a, *Prosopia glandulosa* Torr., Prairie Mesquite; b, *Gymnaclodus dioica* (L.), Kentucky Coffeetree; c, *Robinia hispida* L., Rose Acacia.

The outstanding valuable feature about the family is its use as a soil builder. Nitrogen-fixing bacteria which live in nodules on the roots of the Legumes have the ability to take nitrogen from the air and to make nitrogenous compounds for these bacteria and their host.

Figure 428

115b Ovules attached in two rows on opposite sides of ovary or pod. Flowers irregular. Sepals 2. Petals 4.
Fumitory Family, FUMARIACEAE

Fig.428. *Adlumia fungosa* (Ait.), Climbing Fumitory.

The flowers of this species are greenish purple. The sepals of all members of this family are small and fall early. There are two pairs of petals which differ markedly from each other.

Figure 429

115c Ovules (seeds) attached at center or base of ovary. Flowers regular. Woody plants.
Storax Family, STYRACACEAE

Fig.429. *Styrax americana* Lam., Smooth Storax.

Most of the members of this small family of trees and shrubs are tropical.

115d Ovules many, attached to five ridges (placentae) on the walls of the fleshy, melon-like fruit. Petals on the carpelate flowers almost distinct. Small somewhat palm-like trees; tropical.
Pawpaw Family, CARICACEAE

Figure 430

Fig.430. *Carica papaya* L., Papaya.

This plant must be raised where there is no danger of frost. It is highly regarded for its fruit. It is the source of the drug papain.

137

**116a Ovary with but 2 seeds and 2 cells. Flowers irregular.
Stamens usually 8.   Milkwort Family, POLYGALACEAE**

Fig.431. <u>Polygala</u> <u>alba</u> <u>Nutt.</u>, White Milkwort.

This species is a prairie plant of our western states. The flowers are white.

Figure 431

116b Ovary with 3 or more cells. Figs. 432 to 436. 117

**117a Plants without green coloring matter; living as saprophytes
on humus or decaying roots, etc.   Heath Family, ERICACEAE**

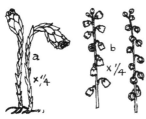

Fig.432. a, <u>Monotropa</u> <u>uniflora</u> L.,
Indian Pipe; b, <u>Pterospora</u> <u>andro-</u>
<u>medea</u> Nutt., Pine Drops.

Someone told us recently of their unsuccessful attempts to transplant Indian Pipe. It could doubtless be done but the decaying organic matter on which it was feeding would need to be brought along also. To raise these plants from seed would likely be easier but even then proper food would be necessary.

Figure 432

117b Plants with green leaves. Figs. 352 and 433 to 436. . .118

**118a Herbs; stamens united by their filaments into a tube.
See Fig. 352.   Mallow Family, MALVACEAE**

118b Woody plants. Figs. 433 to 436. 119

**119a Stamens not united by their filaments. Figs. 433 and
434. . . . . .120**

**119b Stamens united by their filaments into one or more groups.
Figs. 435 and 436. . . . . .121**

**120a Styles 4. Calyx 3 to 7 lobed. Fila-
ments short.   Ebony Family, EBENACEAE**

Fig.433. <u>Diospyros</u> <u>virginiana</u> L., Persimmon.

The fruit of the persimmon is prized for food when thoroughly ripe. It is so bitter as to be long remembered if eaten when green. The wood is unusually hard. The best ebony comes from the heartwood of <u>Diospyros</u> <u>ebenum</u>, a native of India and Ceylon.

Figure 433

138

120b Ovary with but one style. Calyx 4 or 5 lobed.
Heath Family, ERICACEAE

Figure 434

Fig.434. a, <u>Epigaea</u> <u>repens</u> L.,
  Trailing Arbutus; b, <u>Vaccinium</u>
  <u>corymbosum</u> L., Tall Blueberry.

Surely a lot of sentiment centers
around the Trailing Arbutus and who
does not enjoy a piece of blueberry
or huckleberry pie. "Pretty slow
work picking them".

121a Ovary wholly superior. Stamens numerous.
Tea Family, THEACEAE

Figure 435

Fig.435. <u>Stewartia</u> <u>pentagyna</u> L'Hér.,
  Mountain Stewartia.

Tea is made from the leaves of <u>Thea</u>
<u>sinensis</u> L. of this family. It is a shrub or
small tree and is native of China and India.

121b Ovary at most but partly superior.
Storax Family, STYRACACEAE

Figure 436

Fig.436. <u>Halesia</u> <u>carolina</u> L., Silver-bell
  Tree.

A small tree with white flowers. Grows in
woods throughout much of our southeast.

**122a Stamens as many as the corolla lobes and directly in front
(opposite) of them; corolla lobes all alike. Figs. 437 to
439. . . . . .123**

**122b Stamens between the corolla lobes (alternating with them)
or fewer than the lobes. Figs. 440 to 472 . . . . .125**

123a Styles 5, separate or united; fruit dry.
Plumbago Family, PLUMBAGINACEAE

Figure 437

Fig.437. a, <u>Statica</u> <u>armeria</u> L.,
Sea Pink; b, <u>Plumbago</u> <u>capensis</u>
Thunb., Leadwort.

The Leadwort is a delicate but
highly decorative plant used much
in the South. Its flowers are
pale blue or sometimes white. It
is a native of Africa. A red-
flowered species comes from Asia.

123b Style 1. Figs. 438 and 439. 124

Figure 438

**124a Trees or shrubs, often with milky sap.
Sapodilla Family, SAPOTACEAE**

Fig.438. <u>Bumelia</u> <u>lycoides</u> (L.), Carolina
Buckthorn.

The family is a small one and largely
tropical. A number of these exotic species
are raised for ornament.

**124b Herbs; fruit a one-celled capsule with few to many seeds.
Primrose Family, PRIMULACEAE**

Figure 439

Fig.439. a, <u>Dodocatheon</u> <u>meadia</u> L.,
Shooting Star; b, <u>Steironema</u>
<u>ciliatum</u> (L.), Fringed Loose-
strife.

This family produces several
important house plants. It should
not be confused with the Evening
Primrose family for they are quite
different plants.

**125a Corolla regular (the lobes all alike). Figs. 440 to 462.
. . . . .126**

**125b Corolla irregular (the lobes not all alike). Figs. 463 to
472. . . . . .145**

**126a Stamens the same number as the lobes of the corolla.
Figs. 440 to 458 . . . . .127**

**126b Stamens fewer than the lobes of the corolla. Figs. 459
to 462 . . . . .142**

127a Ovary 1, deeply four lobed. Fig. 440 129

Figure 440

127b Ovary 1, not deeply lobed. Figs. 445 to 458. 130

127c Ovaries 2 or sometimes one with two horns; sap usually milky. Figs. 441 and 442. 128

128a Stamens united with each other and with the stigma; styles distinct.   Milkweed Family, ASCLEPIADACEAE

Figure 441

Fig.441. a, <u>Asclepias</u> <u>tuberosa</u> L., Butterfly-weed; b, <u>Vincetoxicum gonocarpos</u> Walt., Large-leaved Angle-pod.

It is the structure of the flower and fruit and not the milky sap that makes a plant a Milkweed. The some 2000 species are scattered pretty much the world over.

128b Stamens not united; no stipules.
Dogbane Family, APOCYNACEAE

Figure 442

Fig.442. a, <u>Apocynum androsaemifolium</u> L., Spreading Dogbane; b,<u>Vinca minor</u> L., Periwinkle.

The Oleander, a very showy shrub or tree, native of Asia, falls here. They (there are 3 species) are raised in the greenhouse in the north but grow out of doors farther south.

129a Leaves alternate; flowers often blue though sometimes yellow or other colors.   Borage Family, BORAGINACEAE

Figure 443

Fig.443. a, <u>Mertensia virginica</u> (L.), Virginia Cowslip; b, <u>Lithospermum canescens</u> (Michx.), Hoary Puccoon.

The family is remembered for its "Forget-me-nots" with their pale blue flowers with white eyes. The plants of this family are usually hairy and the flowers often brilliantly colored.

129b Leaves opposite; stems usually square in cross section.
Mint Family, LABIATAE

141

Figure 444

Fig.444. <u>Isanthus</u> <u>brachiatus</u> (L.),
False Pennyroyal.

Many ornamentals, and some herbs
used for seasoning, fall here. Of the
latter, Garden Sage, Thyme, Peppermint,
Spearmint, Pennyroyal (some rival gum
maker should try it; it's a good one),
Hoarhound, and Summer Savory are
examples.

130a Ovary 1 celled; seed several to many. Figs. 445 and
446 131

130b Ovary more than 1 celled. Figs. 447 to 458 132

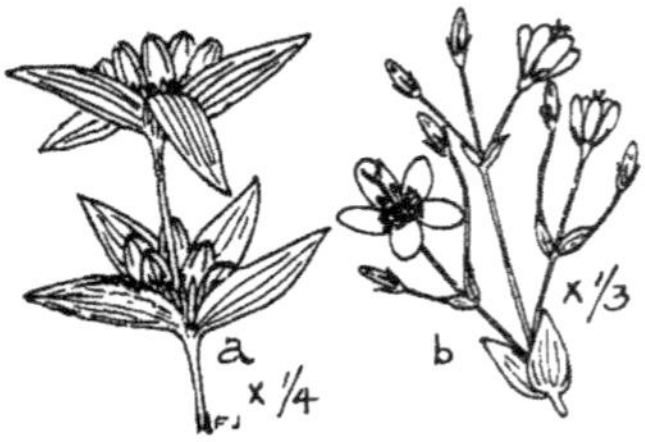

Figure 445

131a Leaves entire and opposite.
(Ovary sometimes partly 2-celled).
Gentian Family, GENTIANACEAE

Fig.445. a, <u>Gentiana</u> <u>andrewsii</u>
Griseb., Closed Gentian; b, <u>Sab-</u>
<u>batia</u> <u>angularis</u> (L.), Rose Pink.

The Fringed Gentian is perhaps
the best known from books. All of
these plants are comparatively rare.

131b Leaves lobed or toothed
or compound.
Water-leaf Family,
HYDROPHYLLACEAE

Fig.446. a, <u>Ellisia</u> <u>nyctelea</u>
L., Nyctelea; b, <u>Hydrophyl-</u>
<u>lum</u> <u>virginicum</u> L., Virginia
Water-leaf.

This family belongs quite
largely to Western North
America.

Figure 447

132a A yellow leafless thread-like plant
twining around other plants on which it
lives parasitically.
Dodder Family, CUSCUTACEAE

Fig.447. <u>Cuscuta</u> <u>gronovii</u> Willd., Love-
vine.

These plants have no chlorophyll and
after they contact their host plant
abandon their roots. About 100 species
are known.

132b Not parasitic. Figs. 448 to 458. 133

142

133a Leaves opposite and stipulate or their bases connected by stipulate lines. Logania Family, LOGANIACEAE

Figure 448

Fig.448. <u>Gelsemium</u> <u>sempervirens</u> (L.), Yellow Jessamine.

An Indian tree of this family produces strychnine. The seeds are used for this purpose. The family is mostly tropical.

133b Leaves alternate or if opposite without stipules or stipular lines. Figs. 449 to 458. 134

134a Stamens not attached to corolla or scarcely so. Figs. 450 and 451. 135

134b Stamens in the notches of the corolla. Low shrubs or herbs. Diapensia Family, DIAPENSIACEAE

Figure 449

Fig.449. <u>Diapensia</u> <u>lapponica</u> L., Diapensia.

It grows well up on our eastern mountains. The flowers are white.

134c Stamens attached to the walls of the corolla. Figs. 452 to 458 136

135a Style 1. Heath Family, ERICACEAE

Figure 450

Fig.450. <u>Azalea</u> <u>lutea</u> L., Flame Azalea.

Few flowers make a finer display than the Azaleas. In April and May out eastern mountains are ablaze with them. Many foreign Azaleas are cultivated.

135b Stigma sessile (style wanting or almost so). Holly Family, AQUIFOLIACEAE

143

Fig.451. <u>Ilex</u> <u>opaca</u> Ait., American Holly.

Most of the Hollies are evergreen. They are prized for ornamental hedges. There are almost 300 species known.

Figure 451

136a Stamens and corolla lobes 4. Figs. 452 and 453. 137

136b Stamens and corolla lobes 5 (or more). Figs. 454 to 458. 138

137a Leaves all arising from the ground, (acaulescent) (a few exceptions), corolla dry and membraneous.
Plantain Family, PLANTAGINACEAE

Fig.452. a, <u>Plantago major</u>, Common Plantain; b, <u>Plantago arenaria</u> W. & K., Sand Plantain.

Some 200 species of Plantains are known. Many of them are bad weeds.

Figure 452

137b Leaves opposite on stems; corolla normal.
Verbena Family, VERBENACEAE

Fig.453. <u>Callicarpa americana</u> L., French Mulberry.

This shrub has pale blue flowers and red-dish-blue fruit. It grows in the southeast.

Figure 453

138a Fruit with 2 or 4 nut-like seeds.
Borage Family, BORAGINACEAE

Fig.454. Heliotropium peruvianum L., Common Heliotrope.

This is a favorite house plant on account of its pleasing odor. The flowers are shades of lavender or sometimes white.

Figure 454

138b Fruit a capsule or pod with few to many seeds. Figs. 455 to 458 139

139a Twining (or trailing) vines, flowers usually showy.
Morning-glory Family, CONVOLVULACEAE

Fig.455. a, Convolvulus sepium L., Hedge Bindweed; b, Ipomoea quamoclit (L.), Cypress Vine.

Some members of the family are prized for ornamentation; some very serious weeds are also included. The sweet-potatoes valued for food are members of the family.

Figure 455

139b Not twining. Figs. 456 to 458 140

140a Styles 2; pod many-seeded; leaves alternate, entire.
Water-leaf Family, HYDROPHYLLACEAE

Fig.456. Nama ovata (Nutt.).

It grows in wet soil and is southern in location. It is a showy plant.

Figure 456

140b Styles but one, though often branched. Figs. 457 and 458. 141

141a Style dividing into 3 linear stigmas.
Phlox Family, POLEMONIACEAE

Fig.457. a, <u>Phlox divaricata</u>
L., Wild Blue Phlox;
b, <u>Polemonium reptans</u> L.,
Greek Valerian; c, <u>Gilia</u>
congesta Hook., Round-
headed Gilia.

Many beautiful garden
plants are included here.

Figure 457

141b Style simple ending in a single terminal stigma.
Potato Family, SOLANACEAE

Figure 458

Fig.458. a, <u>Physalis alkekengi</u> L. Chinese Lantern Plant,
b, <u>Solanum nigrum</u> L., Black Nightshade; c, <u>Datura</u>
<u>stramonium,</u> Jimson-weed.

Some prominent food plants such as "Irish" Potato,
Tomato, Egg Plant, and Peppers belong to the family as does
also Tobacco.

142a Fertile stamens only 2. Figs. 459 and 460 143

142b Fertile stamens 4, in two pairs. Figs. 461 and 462. . .144

143a Herbs with leaves arising at or near the ground.
Plantain Family, PLANTAGINACEAE

Fig.459. <u>Plantago elongata</u> Pursh.,
Slender Plantain.

The plantains have ribbed leaves; the
flowers are small and whitish. They
often grow on poor soil.

Figure 459

143b Trees or shrubs.   **Olive Family, OLEACEAE**

146

Figure 460

Fig.460. a, <u>Syringa</u> <u>vulgaris</u> L., Lilac; b, <u>Fraxinus</u> <u>americana</u> L., White Ash.

Some 30 species of Lilacs, natives of Europe and Asia, are known. They are old favorites for home planting. The flowers are usually of a lavender or purplish shade but white and other colors have been developed.

Figure 461

144a Ovary with 2 cells; each bearing many seeds.

Acanthus Family, ACANTHACEAE

Fig.461. <u>Ruellia</u> <u>ciliosa</u> Pursh., Hairy Ruellia.

This plant resembles the common petunia but is not even closely related to it for petunias belong to the family Solanaceae.

144b Ovary with 2 or 4 cells but with only one seed to a cell.

Verbena Family, VERBENACEAE

Figure 462

Fig.462. <u>Verbena</u> <u>canadensis</u> (L.), Large-flowered Verbena.

Here is a fairly large family. In our region only herbs are represented but the family contains many shrubs and trees as found in warmer regions. Some prized flowering plants and several persistent weeds are abundant with us.

145b Fertile stamens 5.

Figwort Family, SCROPHULARIACEAE

Figure 463

Fig.463. a, <u>Verbascum</u> <u>thapsus</u> L., Common Mullen; b, <u>Verbascum</u> <u>blattaria</u> L., Moth Mullen.

The mullens are native of the old world. There are well over 100 species. Some of these have been introduced as weeds with us.

147

146a With but one seed in each cell of ovary or fruit.
Figs. 464 to 466 147

146b More than one seed in each cell of ovary or fruit.
Figs. 467 to 472 149

147a Ovary with 4 lobes and thread-like style arising at inter-
section of the dividing grooves. Simple opposite leaves; stems
mostly square.   Mint Family, LABIATAE

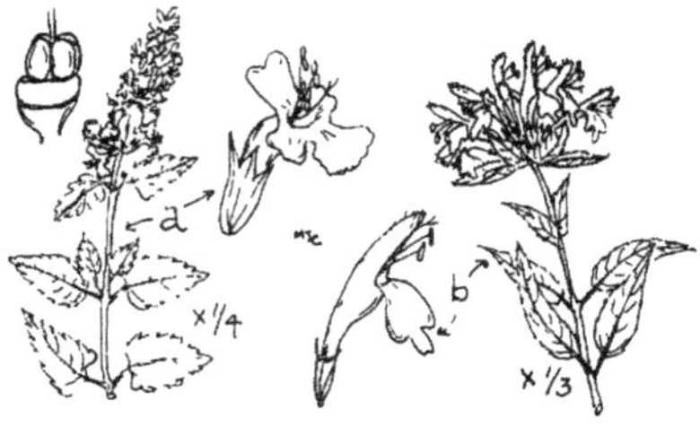

Fig.464. a, Nepeta cataria,
Catnip; b, Monarda fistulosa
L., Horse Mint.

Just why cats should be so
vitally concerned with catnip
is hard to say, but their behavior in its presence shows
that there is some close relationship.

Figure 464

147b Ovary without lobes. Figs. 465 and 466. 148

148a Fruit turned downward, with but 1 cell and 1 seed; leaves
simple, flowers purplish.   Lopseed Family, PHRYMACEAE

Fig.465. Phryma leptostachya L.

The only species of its family.
Fairly common in woods and thickets
throughout the eastern U.S.

Figure 465

148b Fruit not turned downward, 2 to 4-cells each with a single
seed.   Verbena Family, VERBENACEAE

Fig.466. Lippia cuneifolia Steud., Fog-
fruit.

This interesting plant grows in great
abundance in low wet ground. The genus
has many species in the tropics.

Figure 466

149a Ovary 1-celled. Figs. 468 and 469 150

149b   Ovary 2-celled. Figs. 470 to 472. 151

149c   Ovary apparently several-celled (actually 1-celled) due to
    false partitions and diffused placentae.
                          Unicorn-plant Family, MARTYNIACEAE

Fig.467. Martynia louisiana Mill.,
    Unicorn-plant.

    This plant is sometimes raised as
a curiosity but is a native of our
midwest and southwest. The flowers
are whitish and mottled with purple
and yellow.

Figure 467

150a   Whitish, yellowish, or purplish parasites on the roots of
    other plants.   Broomrape Family, OROBANCHACEAE

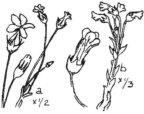

Fig.468. a, Orobanche uniflora L.,
    Cancer-root; b, Orobanche fasciculata
    Nutt., Yellow Cancer-root.

    Parasites are rather unusual among
the seed-bearing plants. A few species
have so completely acquired the
"W.P.A. habit" that they are no longer
able to become independent.

Figure 468

150b   Not parasitic; aquatic plants in which leaves bear minute
    trap-like bladders, or on moist ground.
                          Bladderwort Family, LENTIBULARIACEAE

Fig.469. a, Utricularia vul-
    garis L., Greater Bladder-
    wort; b, Pinguicula vulgar-
    is L., Butterwort.

    Bladderwort, of which there
are several species, grows in
shallow water with its conspicuous yellow flowers arising a few inches above the
surface. Many tiny bladders
serve to trap small aquatic
animals.

Figure 469

151a   Trees, shrubs or woody vines, leaves opposite; seeds
    attached to walls of ovary.
                          Trumpet-creeper Family, BIGNONIACEAE

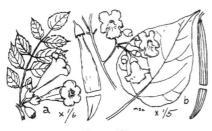

Figure 470

Fig.470. a, <u>Tecoma radicans</u>
(L.), Trumpet-creeper;
b, <u>Catalpa speciosa</u>
Warder., Catalpa.

The Trumpet-creeper with
its large vermilion flowers
makes a very showy vine.
Catalpa wood is valued for
fence posts because of its
resistance to decay. The
showy purple-flowered Brazilian
Jacaranda, much planted in the
South, belongs here.

**151b Seeds attached to central axis; usually herbs. Figs. 471
and 472. . . . . .152**

152a Seeds few, on curved projections.
Acanthus Family, ACANTHACEAE

Fig.471. <u>Dianthera americana</u> L., Dense-flower-
ed Water Willow.

It is common in creeks and other wet places
throughout the middle U. S. The flowers are
lavender or sometimes whitish.

Figure 471

**152b Seeds not borne on curved projections, usually numerous;
filaments of stamens usually covered with hairs.**
Figwort Family, SCROPHULARIACEAE

Figure 472

Fig.472. a, <u>Linaria vul-
garis</u> L. Butter and Eggs;
b, <u>Pedicularis canadensis</u>
L., Lousewort; c, <u>Gerardia
purpurea</u> L., Purple
Gerardia; d, <u>Veronica
peregrina</u> L., Purslane
Speedwell.

Snapdragons, Kenilworth
Ivy, and Foxgloves are among
the well-known ornamentals
of this large family.

A PHYLOGENETIC LIST OF THE FAMILIES OF PLANTS

pinions differ radically among men who are free to think, so it's no wonder that botanists do not always agree on the systematic arrangement of plant families. The list which follows is an attempt to name and arrange the families in a logical order for checking purposes.

The list should help in giving an orderly picture of the entire plant kingdom. If the student will check each family here as he learns to recognize it, he will have a chart showing his progress. An approximate estimate of the number of known species is given for some of the groups in parentheses following the group name.

Division THALLOPHYTA

Sub-division Phycophyta (Algae)

Phylum 1 SCHIZOPHYTA
(Blue Green Algae) - (1500)

Class 1 MYXOPHYCEAE

Order 1 Chroococcales

1. Chroococcaceae
2. Entophysalidaceae

Order 2 Chamaesiphonales

1. Pleurocapsaceae
2. Chamaesiphonaceae

Order 3 Hormogonales

1. Oscillatoriaceae
2. Nostocaceae
3. Scytonemataceae
4. Stigonemataceae
5. Rivulariaceae

Phylum 2 EUGLENAPHYCEAE (350)

Order 1 Euglenales

1. Euglenaceae
2. Colaciaceae
3. Astasiaceae
4. Peranemaceae

Phylum 3 CHLOROPHYTA
(Green Algae) (5500)

Class 1 CHLOROPHYCEAE

Order 1 Volvocales

1. Polyblepharidaceae
2. Chlamydomonadaceae
3. Phacotaceae
4. Volvocaceae
5. Spondylomoraceae
6. Sphaerellaceae

Order 2 Tetrasporales

1. Palmellaceae
2. Tetrasporaceae
3. Chlorangiaceae
4. Coccomyxaceae

Order 3 Ulotrichales

1. Ulotrichaceae
2. Microsporaceae
3. Cylindrocapsaceae
4. Chaetophoraceae
5. Protococcaceae
6. Coleochaetaceae
7. Trentepohliaceae

Order 4 Ulvales

1. Ulvaceae
2. Schizomeridaceae

Order 5 Schizogoniales

1. Schizogoniaceae

Order 6 Cladophorales

1. Cladophoraceae
2. Sphaeropleaceae

Order 7 Oedogoniales

1. Oedogoniaceae

Order 8 Zygnematales

1. Zygnemataceae
2. Mesotaeniaceae
3. Desmidiaceae

Order 9 Chlorococcales

1. Chlorococcaceae
2. Endosphaeraceae
3. Characiaceae
4. Protosiphonaceae
5. Hydrodictyaceae
6. Coelastraceae
7. Oocystaceae
8. Scenedesmaceae

151

Order 10 Siphonales

1. Bryopsidaceae
2. Caulerpaceae
3. Halicystaceae
4. Codiaceae
5. Derbesiaceae
6. Vaucheriaceae
7. Phyllosiphonaceae

Order 11 Siphonocladiales

1. Valoniaceae
2. Dasycladaceae

Phylum 4 CHRYSOPHYTA (6000)

Class 1 HETEROKONTAE

Order 1 Heterochloridales

1. Chloramoebaceae

Order 2 Rhizochloridales

1. Stipitococcaceae

Order 3 Heterocapsales

1. Chlorosaccaceae
2. Mischococcaceae

Order 4 Heterococcales

1. Halosphaeraceae
2. Botryococcaceae
3. Chlorotheciaceae
4. Ophiocytiaceae

Order 5 Heterotrichales

1. Tribonemataceae
2. Monociliaceae

Order 6 Heterosiphonales

1. Botrydiaceae

Class 2 CHRYSOPHYCEAE

Order 1 Chrysomonadales

1. Chromulinaceae
2. Mallomonadaceae
3. Syncryptaceae
4. Synuraceae
5. Ochromonadinaceae
6. Physomonadaceae

Order 2 Rhizochryidales

1. Rhizochrysidaceae

Order 3 Chrysocapsales

1. Chrysocapsaceae
2. Hydruraceae

Order 4 Chrysotrichales

1. Phaeothamniaceae

Class 3 BACILLARIEAE
(Diatoms) (5000)

Order 1 Centrales

1. Coscinodiscaceae

2. Eupodiscaceae
3. Rhizosoleniaceae
4. Chaetoceraceae
5. Biddulphiaceae
6. Anaulaceae

Order 2 Pennales

1. Tabellariaceae
2. Meridionaceae
3. Diatomaceae
4. Fragilariaceae
5. Eunotiaceae
6. Achnanthaceae
7. Naviculaceae
8. Gomphonemataceae
9. Cymbellaceae
10. Nitzschiaceae
11. Surirellaceae

Phylum 5 PYRROPHYTA (975)

Class 1 DINOPHYCEAE

Order 1 Gymnodiniales

Order 2 Peridiniales

Order 3 Dinophysidales

Order 4 Rhizodiniales

Order 5 Dinocapsales

Order 6 Dinotrichales

Order 7 Dinococcales

Phylum 6 PHAEOPHYTA
(Brown Algae) (1000)

Class 1 ISOGENERATAE

Order 1 Ectocarpales

1. Ectocarpaceae

Order 2 Sphacelariales

1. Sphacelariaceae

Order 3 Tilopteridales

1. Tilopteridaceae

Order 4 Cutleriales

1. Cutleriaceae

Order 5 Dictyotales

1. Dictyotaceae

Class 2 HETEROGENERATAE

Order 1 Chordariales

1. Chordariaceae
2. Leathesiaceae

Order 2 Sporochnales

1. Sporochnaceae

152

Order 3 Desmarestiales

1. Desmarestiaceae

Order 4 Punctariales

1. Scytosiphonaceae
2. Asperococcaceae
3. Coilodesmaceae
4. Punctariaceae

Order 5 Dictyosiphonales

1. Dictyosiphonaceae

Order 6 Laminariales (Kelps)

1. Chordaceae
2. Phyllariaceae
3. Laminariaceae
4. Alariaceae
5. Lessoniaceae

Class 3 CYCLOSPOREAE

Order 1 Fucales

1. Fucaceae
2. Sargassaceae

Phylum 7 RHODOPHYTA
(Red Algae) (2500)

Class 1 RHODOPHYCEAE

Order 1 Bangiales

1. Bangiaceae

Order 2 Nemalionales

1. Chantransiaceae
2. Batrachospermaceae
3. Bonnemaisonaceae
4. Helminthocladiaceae
5. Chaetangiaceae

Order 3 Gelidiales

1. Gelidiaceae

Order 4 Cryptonemiales

1. Dumontiaceae
2. Squamariaceae
3. Corallinaceae
4. Endocladiaceae

Order 5 Gigartinales

1. Cruoriaceae
2. Gracilariaceae
3. Plocamiaceae
4. Rissoellaceae
5. Solieriaceae
6. Rhodophyllidaceae
7. Hypneaceae
8. Gigartinaceae

Order 6 Rhodymeniales

1. Champiaceae
2. Rhodymeniaceae

Order 7 Ceramiales

1. Ceramiaceae

2. Delesseriaceae
3. Rhodomelaceae

Phylum 8 CHAROPHYTA (200)

Class 1 CHAROPHYCEAE

Order 1 Charales

1. Characeae

Phylum 9 LICHENES
(Lichens) (15,000)

Order 1 Basidiolichenes

Order 2 Ascolichenes

1. Caliciaceae
2. Graphidaceae
3. Lecanactidaceae
4. Gyalectaceae
5. Lecideaceae
6. Psoraceae
7. Baeomycetaceae
8. Cladoniaceae
9. Stereocaulaceae
10. Collemaceae
11. Pyrenopsidaceae
12. Ephebaceae
13. Pannariaceae
14. Stictaceae
15. Peltigeraceae
16. Gyrophoraceae
17. Lecanoraceae
18. Pertusariaceae
19. Parmeliaceae
20. Teloschistaceae
21. Physciaceae
22. Verrucariaceae
23. Pyrenulaceae
24. Dermatocarpaceae
25. Endocarpaceae
26. Leprariaceae

Phylum 10 SCHIZOMYCETES (Bacteria)

Order 1 Eubacteriales (True Bacteria)

1. Nitrobacteriaceae
2. Coccaceae
3. Spirillaceae
4. Bacteriaceae
5. Bacillaceae

Order 2 Actinomycetales

1. Actinomycetaceae
2. Mycobacteriaceae

Order 3 Chlamydobacteriales

1. Chlamydobacteriaceae

Order 4 Thiobacteriales

1. Rhodobacteriaceae
2. Beggiatoaceae
3. Achromatiaceae

Order 5 Myxobacteriales

1. Myxobacteriaceae

Order 6 Spirochaetales

  1. Spirochaetaceae

Order 7 Caulobacteriales

  1. Gallionellaceae

Order 8 Rickettsiales

  1. Rickettsiaceae

Phylum 11 MYXOTHALLOPHYTA (450)

Class 1 MYXOMYCETAE

Order 1 Endosporales

  1. Trichiaceae
  2. Lycogalaceae
  3. Cribrariaceae
  4. Stemonitaceae
  5. Physaraceae

Order 2 Exosporales

  1. Ceratiomyxaceae

Class 2 PHYTOMYXINAE

Order 1 Plasmodiophorales

  1. Plasmodiophoraceae

Class 3 ACRASIEAE

Order 1 Acrasiales

  1. Acrasiaceae
  2. Dictyosteliaceae

Phylum 12 EUMYCETES
(True Fungi) (75,000)

Class 1 PHYCOMYCETES
(Algal-like Fungi) (15,000)

Order 1 Chytridales

  1. Rhizidiaceae
  2. Olpidiaceae
  3. Synchytriaceae
  4. Cladochytriaceae
  5. Woroninaceae

Order 2 Blastocladiales

  1. Blastocladiaceae

Order 3 Monoblepharidales

  1. Monoblepharidaceae

Order 4 Ancylistales

  1. Ancylistaceae

Order 5 Saprolegniales

  1. Saprolegniaceae
  2. Leptomitaceae
  3. Pythiaceae

Order 6 Peronosporales

  1. Peronosporaceae
  2. Albuginaceae

Order 7 Mucorales

  1. Mucoraceae
  2. Mortierellaceae
  3. Choanephoraceae
  4. Chaetocladiaceae
  5. Piptocephalidaceae

Order 8 Entomophthorales

  1. Entomophthoraceae
  2. Basidiobolaceae

Class 2 ASCOMYCETES
(Sac Fungi) (24,000)

Order 1 Saccharomycetales

  1. Saccharomycetaceae
  2. Endomycetaceae

Order 2 Aspergilliales

  1. Gymnoascaceae
  2. Aspergillaceae
  3. Onygenaceae
  4. Trichcomaceae
  5. Myriangiaceae.
  6. Elaphomycetaceae
  7. Terfeziaceae

Order 3 Erysiphales

  1. Erysiphaceae
  2. Perisporiaceae
  3. Microthyriaceae

Order 4 Hysteriales

  1. Hypodermataceae
  2. Dichaenaceae
  3. Ostropaceae
  4. Hysteriaceae
  5. Acrospermaceae

Order 5 Phacidiales

  1. Stictidaceae
  2. Tryblidiaceae
  3. Phacidiaceae

Order 6 Pezizales

  1. Pyronemaceae
  2. Pezizaceae
  3. Ascobolaceae
  4. Helotiaceae
  5. Mollisiaceae
  6. Celidiaceae
  7. Patellariaceae
  8. Cenangiaceae
  9. Cordieritidaceae
  10. Cyttariaceae
  11. Caliciaceae

Order 7 Tuberales

  1. Tuberaceae

Order 8 Helvellales

  1. Geoglossaceae
  2. Helvellaceae
  3. Rhizinaceae

Order 9 Exoascales

1. Exoascaceae
2. Ascocorticiaceae

Order 10 Hypocreales

1. Hypocreaceae

Order 11 Sphaeriales

1. Chaetomiaceae
2. Sordariaceae
3. Sphaeriaceae
4. Ceratostomataceae ·
5. Cucubitariaceae
6. Coryneliaceae
7. Amphisphaeriaceae
8. Lophiostomataceae
9. Mycosphaerellaceae
10. Pleosporaceae
11. Massariaceae
12. Gnomoniaceae
13. Clypeosphaeriaceae
14. Valsaceae
15. Melanconidaceae
16. Diatrypaceae
17. Melogrammataceae
18. Xylariaceae

Order 12 Dothidiales

1. Dothidiaceae

Order 13 Laboulbeniales

1. Peyritschiellaceae
2. Laboulbeniaceae
3. Zodiomycetaceae

Class 3 BASIDIOMYCETES
(Club Fungi) (20,000)

Order 1 Ustilaginales

1. Ustilaginaceae
2. Tilletiaceae

Order 2 Uredinales

1. Endophyllaceae
2. Melampsoraceae
3. Pucciniaceae
4. Coleosporaceae

Order 3 Tremellales

1. Auriculariaceae
2. Tremellaceae

Order 4 Hymenomycetales

1. Dacryomycetaceae
2. Exobasidiaceae
3. Hypochnaceae
4. Thelephoraceae
5. Clavariaceae
6. Hydnaceae
7. Polyporaceae
8. Boletaceae
9. Agaricaceae

Order 5 Gasteromycetales

1. Lycoperdaceae

2. Phallaceae
3. Clathraceae

Phylum 13 BRYOPHYTA (3,000)

Class 1 HEPATICAE (Liverworts)

Order 1 Jungermanniales

1. Ptilidiaceae
2. Lepidoziaceae
3. Calypogeiaceae
4. Cephaloziaceae
5. Cephaloziellaceae
6. Harpanthaceae
7. Jungermanniaceae
8. Marsupellaceae
9. Plagiochilaceae
10. Scapaniaceae
11. Porellaceae
12. Radulaceae
13. Frullaniaceae
14. Lejeuneaceae

Order 2 Metzgeriales

1. Fossombroniaceae
2. Pelliaceae
3. Haplolaenaceae
4. Pallaviciniaceae
5. Metzgeriaceae
6. Aneuraceae

Order 3 Marchantiales

1. Marchantiaceae
2. Rebouliaceae
3. Ricciaceae

Order 4 Sphaerocarpales

1. Sphaerocarpaceae

Order 5 Anthocerotales

1. Anthocerotaceae

Class 2 MUSCI (Mosses)

Order 1 Sphagnales

1. Sphagnaceae

Order 2 Andreaeales

1. Andreaeaceae

Order 3 Bryales

1. Tetraphidaceae
2. Polytrichaceae
3. Fissidentaceae
4. Archidiaceae
5. Ditrichaceae
6. Seligeriaceae
7. Dicranaceae
8. Leucobryaceae
9. Calymperaceae
10. Encalyptaceae
11. Buxbaumiaceae
12. Pottiaceae
13. Grimmiaceae
14. Ephemeraceae
15. Disceliaceae

16. Funariaceae
17. Splachnaceae
18. Schistostegaceae
19. Orthotrichaceae
20. Timmiaceae
21. Aulacomniaceae
22. Bartramiaceae
23. Bryaceae
24. Mniaceae
25. Hypnaceae
26. Leskeaceae
27. Hookeriaceae
28. Neckeraceae
29. Leucodontaceae
30. Cryphaeaceae
31. Fabroniaceae
32. Fontinalaceae

Phylum 14 PTERIDOPHYTA (Ferns)

Order 1 Filicales (4,000)

1. Hymenophyllaceae
2. Polypodiaceae
3. Schizaeaceae
4. Osmundaceae
5. Ophioglossaceae
6. Marsileaceae
7. Salviniaceae
8. Cyatheaceae

Order 2 Equisetales (30)

1. Equisetaceae

Order 3 Lycopodiales (500)

1. Lycopodiaceae
2. Selaginellaceae
3. Isoetaceae

Phylum 15 SPERMATOPHYTA
(Seed-bearing Plants)

Class 1 GYMNOSPERMAE (500)

Order 1 Cycadales

1. Cycadaceae

Order 2 Ginkgoales

1. Ginkgoaceae

Order 3 Coniferales

1. Taxaceae
2. Pinaceae

Order 4 Gnetales

1. Gnetaceae

Class 2 ANGIOSPERMAE (130,000)

Subclass Monocotyledoneae ("Monocots")

Order 1 Pandanales

1. Typhaceae
2. Sparganiaceae

Order 2 Najadales

1. Najadaceae

2. Scheuchzeriaceae
3. Alismaceae
4. Hydrocharitaceae

Order 3 Graminales

1. Gramineae
2. Cyperaceae

Order 4 Palmales

1. Palmaceae

Order 5 Cyclanthales

1. Cyclanthaceae

Order 6 Arales

1. Araceae
2. Lemnaceae

Order 7 Xeridales

1. Eriocaulaceae
2. Xyridaceae
3. Mayacaceae
4. Commelinaceae
5. Bromeliaceae
6. Pontederiaceae

Order 8 Liliales

1. Juncaceae
2. Liliaceae
3. Haemodoraceae
4. Dioscoreaceae
5. Amaryllidaceae
6. Iridaceae

Order 9 Scitaminales

1. Marantaceae
2. Musaceae
3. Cannaceae

Order 10 Orchidales

1. Burmanniaceae
2. Orchidaceae

Subclass Dicotyledoneae ("Dicots")

Order 11 Casuarinales

1. Casuarinaceae

Order 12 Piperales

1. Saururaceae

Order 13 Juglandales

1. Juglandaceae

Order 14 Myricales

1. Myricaceae

Order 15 Salicales

1. Salicaceae

Order 16 Fagales

1. Betulaceae
2. Fagaceae

Order 17 Urticales

   1. Urticaceae

Order 18 Santalales

   1. Santalaceae
   2. Loranthaceae

Order 19 Proteales

   1. Proteaceae

Order 20 Aristolochiales

   1. Aristolochiaceae

Order 21 Polygonales

   1. Polygonaceae

Order 22 Chenopodiales

   1. Chenopodiaceae
   2. Amaranthaceae
   3. Phytolaccaceae
   4. Nyctaginaceae
   5. Illecebraceae
   6. Aizoaceae
   7. Basellaceae

Order 23 Caryophyllales

   1. Caryophyllaceae
   2. Portulacaceae

Order 24 Rananculales

   1. Ceratophyllaceae
   2. Nymphaeaceae
   3. Ranunculaceae
   4. Magnoliaceae
   5. Calycanthaceae
   6. Anonaceae
   7. Menispermaceae
   8. Berberidaceae
   9. Lauraceae

Order 25 Papaverales

   1. Papaveraceae
   2. Fumariaceae
   3. Cruciferae
   4. Capparidaceae
   5. Resedaceae

Order 26 Sarraceniales

   1. Sarraceniaceae
   2. Droseraceae

Order 27 Rosales

   1. Podostemaceae
   2. Crassulaceae
   3. Parnassiaceae
   4. Saxifragaceae
   5. Pittosporaceae
   6. Hamamelidaceae
   7. Platanaceae
   8. Rosaceae
   9. Leguminosae

Order 28 Geraniales

   1. Linaceae

   2. Oxalidaceae
   3. Tropaeolaceae
   4. Geraniaceae
   5. Zygophyllaceae
   6. Rutaceae
   7. Simaroubaceae
   8. Meliaceae
   9. Polygalaceae
  10. Euphorbiaceae
  11. Callitrichaceae

Order 29 Sapindales

   1. Buxaceae
   2. Empetraceae
   3. Limnanthaceae
   4. Anacardiaceae
   5. Cyrillaceae
   6. Aquifoliaceae
   7. Celastraceae
   8. Staphyleaceae
   9. Aceraceae
  10. Sapindaceae
  11. Balsaminaceae

Order 30 Rhamnales

   1. Rhamnaceae
   2. Vitaceae

Order 31 Malvales

   1. Tiliaceae
   2. Malvaceae

Order 32 Violales

   1. Theaceae
   2. Tamaricaceae
   3. Hypericaceae
   4. Elatinaceae
   5. Cistaceae
   6. Violaceae
   7. Passifloraceae
   8. Caricaceae
   9. Loasaceae

Order 33 Begoniales

   1. Begoniaceae

Order 34 Opuntiales

   1. Cactaceae

Order 35 Myrtales

   1. Thymelaceae
   2. Eleagnaceae
   3. Lythraceae
   4. Myrtaceae
   5. Melastomaceae
   6. Onagraceae
   7. Haloragidaceae

Order 36 Umbellales

   1. Araliaceae
   2. Umbelliferae
   3. Cornaceae

Order 37 Ericales

   1. Ericaceae
   2. Diapensiaceae

Order 38 Primulales

1. Plumbaginaceae
2. Primulaceae

Order 39 Ebenales

1. Sapotaceae
2. Ebenaceae
3. Styracaceae

Order 40 Gentianales

1. Oleaceae
2. Loganiaceae
3. Gentianaceae
4. Apocynaceae
5. Asclepiadaceae

Order 41 Polemoniales

1. Cuscutaceae
2. Convolvulaceae
3. Polemoniaceae
4. Hydrophyllaceae
5. Boraginaceae
6. Verbenaceae

7. Labiatae
8. Solanaceae
9. Scrophulariaceae
10. Lentibulariaceae
11. Orobanchaceae
12. Bignoniaceae
13. Martyniaceae
14. Gesneriaceae
15. Acanthaceae
16. Phrymaceae

Order 42 Plantaginales

1. Plantaginaceae

Order 43 Rubiales

1. Rubiaceae
2. Caprifoliaceae
3. Valerianaceae
4. Dipsacaceae

Order 44 Campanulales

1. Cucurbitaceae
2. Campanulaceae
3. Lobeliaceae
4. Compositae

158

INDEX AND PICTURED GLOSSARY

Figure 473

Figure 474

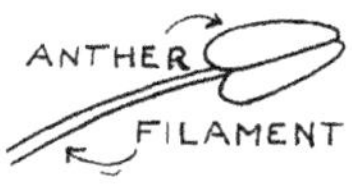

Figure 475

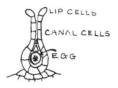

Figure 476

Figure 477

Figure 478

Figure 479

Figure 480

Figure 481

Figure 482

Figure 483

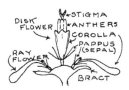

Figure 484

Compound Leaf, one divided into several leaflets.
Conceptacle, a cavity containing reproductive cells.
Conidia, asexual cells, budded-off from the end of an elongated cell, the conidiophore. (Fig. 485)

Conidiophore, cell producing conidia. (Fig. 485)

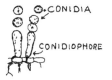

Figure 485

Cotyledons, seed-leaves, containing stored food. (Fig. 486)

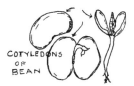

Figure 486

D

Figure 487

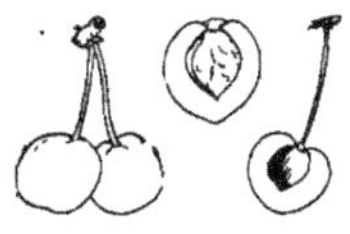

E

Figure 488

F

Flagellum, elongated
thread-like structure
for locomotion.
(Fig. 489)

Figure 489

Flame Azalea 143
Flax Family 126
Floating Moss 86
Floerkea 126
Florida Moss 96
Flowering Fern Family 88
Flowering Plants 8
Flower-of-an-Hour 115
Fog-fruit 148
Follicle, a dry fruit of
but one carpel which
opens on its ventral
side. (Fig. 490)

Figure 490

Fontinalaceae 85
Fontinalis 85
Forked Chickweed 108
Forking Whitlow-wort 108
Forsstraemia 85
Fossil plants 5
Fossombriaceae 72
Fossombronia 72
Fossombroniaceae 72
Four-o'clock Family 108
Foxglove 150
Fragilaria 29
Fragilariaceae 29
Fraxinus 147
French Mulberry 144
Fringed Gentian 142
Fringed Loosetrife 140
Fringe-tree 129
Frog's Bit 97
Frog's Bit Family 97
Frond, leaf-like part.
Frullania 77
Frullaniaceae 77
Frustule 26,27
Frustulia 29
Fucaceae 39
Fuchsia 131
Fucus 39
Fuligo 52
Fumariaceae 117,137
Fumitory Family 117,137
Funaria 82
Funariaceae 82
Funariales 82
Fungi 8,47

G

Galanthus 98
Galium 136
Gallionella 48
Gallionellaceae 47
Gametangium, organ bear-
ing gametes; reproduc-
tive organ.
Gametophyte, sexual stage
of plant; bearing
gametes.
Garden Heliotrope 135
Gardenia 136
Garden Mignonette 116
Garden Nasturtium 122
Garden Pink 121
Garlic 96
Gasteromycetales 69
Gaura 131
Geaster 69
Gelidiaceae 40
Gelidium 40
Gelsemium 143
Geminella 24
Gemma, asexual bud-like
reproductive body.
Gentiana 142
Gentianaceae 142
Gentian Family 142
Genus 7
Geoglossaceae 60
Geoglossum 60
Georgia 78
Geraniaceae 126
Geranium Family 126
Gerardia 150
Geum 113
Giant Cactus 132
Giant Snowdrop 98
Gigartina 42
Gigartinaceae 42
Gigartinales 42
Gilia 146
Gills 68
Ginkgo 90
Ginkgoaceae 90
Ginkgo Family 90
Ginseng 132
Ginseng Family 131
Glandular Croton 125
Gleba 70
Gleocapsa 12
Gleocystis 19
Globe Amaranth 108
Glomerate Sedge 92
Glomerella 64
Glumes 92
Gnomoniaceae 64
Golden Cactus 132
Golden Corydalis 117
Golden Currant 133
Golenkinia 21
Gomphonema 30
Gomphonemataceae 29
Gomphrena 108
Gonium 18
Gooseberry 113,133
Goosefoot Family 108

Gourd 129
Gourd Family 129,134
Gramineae 92
Grape Family 118
Grape Fern 88
Graphidaceae 44
Graphis 44
Grasses 92
Grass Family 92
Grass-of-Parnassus
Family 119
Greater Bladderwort 149
Greater Caltrop 126
Greater Duckweed 91
Greek Valerian 146
Green Algae 15
Green Dragon 93
Green-felt 16
Green Milkweed 121
Grimmia 81
Grimmiaceae 81
Grinnellia 43
Ground-pine 89
Guignardia 64
Gum 130
Gymnaclodus 137
Gymnodiniales 31
Gymnodinium 31
Gymnospermae 89
Gymnosperms 90
Gyromitra 60

H

Haemodoraceae 98
Hair-cap Moss 78
Hairy Ruellia 147
Hakea 107
Halesia 139
Haloragidaceae 130
Halosphaeraceae 33
Hamamelidaceae 103,113
Hamamelis 103
Hantzshia 30
Haploid, having the half
number of chromosomes
Haplolaenaceae 73
Haplolepideae 78
Haplospora 35
Harebell 135
Harpanshis 75
Harpanthaceae 75
Heath 116
Heather 127
Heath Family 127,138,
139,143
Hedge Bindweed 145
Hedge Mustard 128
Helianthemum 116
Heliotrope 135
Heliotropium 145
Helminthocladiaceae 41
Helotiaceae 59
Helvella 60
Helvellaceae 60
Helvellales 60
Hemibasidii 65

164

Figure 491

I

Figure 492

Figure 493

J

K

L

N

Figure 495

O

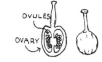

Figure 496

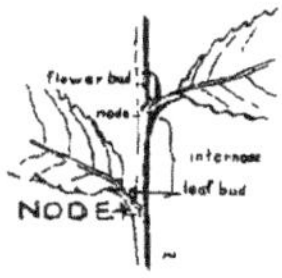

P

Figure 497

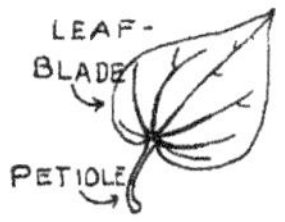

Figure 498

Panicle, a loose inflorescence with the pedicels branched. (Fig. 499)

Figure 499

Papillae, small projecting parts.
Paraphyses, sterile cells or threads among fruiting bodies.
Parietal placenta 119
Pedicel, stem supporting a flower or fruit. (Fig. 500)

Figure 500

Peltate, leaf in which petiole attaches inside the margin. (Fig. 501)

Figure 501

Pepo, fleshy fruit of the melon or pumpkin type 134
Perfoliate, leaf surrounding the stem. (Fig. 502)

Figure 502

Perianth, sepals and petals taken collectively; both calyx and corolla. (Fig. 503)

Figure 503

Pericarp, outer covering of a fruiting body.

Peristome, fringe of teeth surrounding the mouth of moss capsules. (Fig. 504)

Figure 504

Perithecium, a closed fruiting body, in the fungi 58: Fig. 505

Figure 505

Petal, one of the parts composing the corolla. (Fig. 506)

Figure 506

Figure 507

Pinnately Veined, all
   the principal veins of
   a leaf standing later-
   ally on both sides of
   the midrib. (Fig. 508)

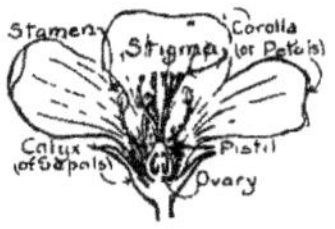

Figure 508

Figure 509

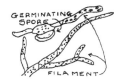

Figure 510

Q

R

Raceme, an inflores-
cence as pictured.
(Fig. 511)

Figure 511

Figure 512

Rhizome, an under-ground
stem for storing food,
(a) or growing new
plants. (b) (Fig. 513)

Figure 513

S

Figure 514

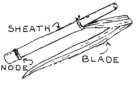

Figure 515

Figure 516

Figure 517

Figure 518

Stamen, pollen bearing
  organ in flower.
  (Fig. 519)

Figure 519

Staminate Flower, male
  flower with stamens
  but no pistil.
  (Fig. 519)
Stigma, part of pistil
  that receives the pol-
  len. (Fig. 520)

Figure 520

Stipe, a short stalk as
  the stem of a mush-
  room.
Stipules, leaf-like
  outgrowths at base
  of petiole.
  (Fig. 521)

Figure 521

Style, part of pistil
  that supports the
  stigma. (See Fig.
  520)
Superior Ovary, arising
  above the calyx 94,109,
  134: (Fig. 522)

Figure 522

Symbiont, either member
  of two species living
  together

T

Teleutospore, thick-
  walled winter spore.
  (Fig. 523)

Figure 523

Figure 524

U

Figure 525

V

Figure 526

W

Figure 527

X

Y

Z

Figure 528

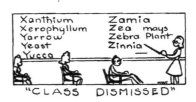

"CLASS DISMISSED"

174

CPSIA information can be obtained at www.ICGtesting.com
Printed in the USA
BVOW06s1739120715

408469BV00012B/123/P

9 781258 475666